KEEPING THE FAITH

Keeping the Faith

AFRICAN AMERICAN SERMONS OF LIBERATION

Edited by James Haskins

INTRODUCTION BY MAYA ANGELOU

WELCOME RAIN PUBLISHERS   New York

KEEPING THE FAITH:
AFRICAN AMERICAN SERMONS OF LIBERATION
Edited with a preface by James Haskins, introduction by Maya Angelou
All rights reserved.

Preface copyright © 2002 by James Haskins
Introduction copyright © 2002 by Maya Angelou

Copyright information for the individual sermons is available
on the last page of the book.

Library of Congress CIP data available from the publisher.

Direct any inquiries to
Welcome Rain Publishers LLC,
23 West 26th Street
New York, NY 10010

ISBN 1-56649-192-4
Printed in the United States of America
by HAMILTON PRINTING COMPANY

Design by Cindy LaBreacht

First Edition: March 2002
1 3 5 7 9 10 8 6 4 2

To Christine Vargas and Jennifer Noughton

With a special dedication to Cathy

ON THE AUDIO CD

1. Introduction
2. James Weldon Johnson, "Go Down Death" (read by James Earl Jones)
3. Introduction
4. Jeremiah Wright, "A Broken Life"
5. Introduction
6. C.L. Franklin, "The Eagle Stirreth Her Nest"
7. Introduction
8. Martin Luther King, Jr., "We Must Work"
9. Introduction
10. Gardner C. Taylor, "Jesus Is the Centerpiece of Our Faith"
11. Introduction
12. Wyatt Tee Walker, "Choose Ye This Day"
13. Introduction
14. W. Franklyn Richardson II, "What Do the Ashes Say?"
15. Introduction
16. Adam Clayton Powell, Jr., "Keep the Faith, Baby!"
17. Introduction
18. Katie G. Cannon, "Living the Life of Jubilee"
19. Introduction
20. Jasper Williams, Jr., "A Good Soldier: A Eulogy of C.L. Franklin"

Introductions are read by the Reverend Sharone Davis-Smith

Contents

ACKNOWLEDGMENTS

A special thanks to Anne Jordan for her invaluable assistance in the compilation of this anthology and to Dr. Wyatt Tee Walker, whose wise counsel and guidance were invaluable in selecting the sermons for this volume, choosing from an extraordinary group of ministers and visionaries. Thanks to Carla Blount and to Betty Burditte, assistant to Dr. Maya Angelou, and special acknowledgment to Maya, who found this project important enough to contribute the introduction, a very important statement in which she manages to convey a thorough understanding of the African-American oral/political tradition in a few words. Thanks to John Weber, publisher of this work, who saw from the start the necessity of adding a new voice to some very old issues and questions. And finally, thank you to Victoria W. McGoey, Michele Rubin, Yvonne Knight, Norah Piehl, Reverend Constance P. George, and Naeemah Clark.

Welcome Rain Publishers would like to thank Reverend Sharone Davis-Smith for her tireless work and unending faith in this book.

Preface

JAMES HASKINS

Preacher read Scripture,
The Word, the past.
Preacher conjure agos, to-bes,
Can-bes, must-bes,
Paint strife, life—

Amen!

Preacher feed us, lead us,
Moses out of Egypt,
Martin out of Selma,
"Let my people go,"
To the mountain, to the dream—

Amen!

Preacher rock us in the cradle,
Preacher lead us to the river,
Preacher swing low, sing low sweet chariot,
Sing the Word, our word,
Our world,
Forever and ever—

Amen!

A.D. Jordan[1]

African American preachers were and are much more than mere
purveyors of the Word of God. They are cultural and social
historians, repositories of traditions reaching far back into the past and
across oceans, and leaders in protesting the inequities and tribulations

---

1. Jordan, A.D. "Preacher." 2001. Used with permission of the author.

of life. Their ministries, regardless of denomination, have always grappled with all of existence. "African-American religion," Dr. Terry Matthews writes, deals "with life as blacks lived it. It [is] about pain and sorrow, sin and shortcoming, pardon and joy, praise and thanksgiving, grace and hope."[2]

When the first slaves were dragged from their homes and bound into captivity, shackled and shipped to the New World, their masters thought they had stripped them of their lives and identities. Yet, when the slave owners imposed their religion—Christianity—upon them, those slaves added to that religion the treasures that could not be stolen from them. Even today, the storytelling techniques and rhythms of the akete (talking) drums of their homelands pervade African American hymns and sermons. C.C. Lovelace's "The Sermon," for example, utilizes the call-and-response so typical of the performances of the griots of the west coast of Africa in which a spoken or sung line elicits a choral response from the audience.

Forbidden to learn to read or write, the early black preachers and ministers of the New World assumed the role that the griot held in West Africa. African griots (griotte, fem.) were the rhythmic storytellers and town criers of West African society. They "are rightly referred to as the archives and libraries of this part of Africa," Wolfgang Bender writes, "They were the interpreters of current politics, transmitting messages and orders from the governing power to the people."[3] The griot played an important role in African society, and by assuming many of the same functions and using oral techniques harking back to them, preachers also became vital in making the black churches "the foundations of Afro-American culture."[4]

2. Matthews, Dr. Terry. Lecture Twelve: The Religion of the Slaves. http://www.wfu.edu/~matthetl/perspectives/twelve.html. Accessed: 4/22/01: 6.
3. Bender, Wolfgang. Sweet Mothers. Chicago: University of Chicago Press, 1991: 17-18.
4. Ruboteau, Albert J. Slave Rebellion. As quoted in: The Oxford Companion to African American Literature, William L. Andrews, Frances Smith Foster, & Trudier Harris, eds. New York: Oxford University Press, 1997: 648.

For blacks in the early United States, church services were an important part of life, and over the years two distinct but overlapping traditions emerged: the slave preachers or "exhorters" who brought color and drama to their imaginative retelling of the trials and triumphs of the Israelites in the Bible, and the learned tradition.[5]

As with the performances of the griots earlier, the sermons of the early preachers, particularly those of the "exhorters" who emerged during the wave of religious feeling called the Great Awakening that swept the country around 1740, were "lively, uplifting affairs, complete with music, chanting, and spiritual possessions . . . .[6] This same emotional tradition emerges in the sermons of more modern preachers such as C.C. Lovelace, Dr. Martin Luther King, Jr., and in the poetry of James Weldon Johnson.

The "learned" tradition stems from those "preachers who preached from a manuscript or notes,"[7] preachers in the antebellum South who, despite the ban on reading and writing, managed to acquire learning, those in the North who were able to gain an education, and those who have followed and maintained that tradition. Their sermons were and are no less uplifting than the sermons of the more emotional exhorters. Many, in their sermons, shored up the hopes for equality for African Americans and helped those hopes be realized. One modern example is Wyatt Tee Walker's "Lock-Jaw Lions," a scholarly but emotive discourse on the hymn "Daniel in the Lions' Den" which, he writes, expresses both spiritual and worldly hopes: "the faith-response was that God delivered Daniel from the lions' den, so would He deliver his children of darker hue from the lions' den of slavery and twentieth century racism."[8]

---

5. Andrews, William L., Frances Smith Foster & Trudier Harris, eds. "Sermons and Preaching." The Oxford Companion to African American Literature. New York: Oxford University Press, 1997: 648.
6. Jones, K. Maurice. Say It Loud! Brookfield, CT: The Millbrook Press, 1994: 22-23.
7. Andrews: 648.
8. Walker, Wyatt Tee. Spirits That Dwell in Deep Woods II: The Prayer and Praise Hymns of the Black Religious Experience. New York: Martin Luther King Fellows Press, 1988: 77.

On a more pragmatic level, many of the older sermons and spirituals also contained covert messages concerning actual deliverance: A lyric like "I ain't got long to stay here," from the spiritual "Deep River," superficially meant that a slave was about to die and looked forward to life in the Promised Land, or Jordan. However, for many slaves, the song often signaled the local presence of Underground Railroad conductors like Harriet Tubman.[9]

In more recent times, the messages of freedom and protest by African American ministers have become more overt, ranging from the calls for equality in the sermons of Martin Luther King Jr. to the Rev. W. Franklyn Richardson's inspiring bolsterer of faith, "Holding On To Your Song."

Early preachers inspired their listeners to have hope for this world and the next, and at the same time, often aided them in attaining that more earthly hope. And many of those communicating that were black women, both free and enslaved. Just as in West African society where there were female griots—griottes—women have played and do play important roles in the black churches of America, although, at times, in the face of patriarchal opposition: black women were not 'officially recognized or ordained as preachers' until the late nineteenth or early twentieth century, though slave women undoubtedly 'preached in clandestine services.' Unlike their male counterparts, they were required to take 'sublimated paths to the ministry' as exhorters, teachers, missionaries, evangelists, religious writers, and wives of clergymen.[10]

Although there were many early self-proclaimed black female preachers, they were not officially recognized by the early African American churches. In the late 1800s, women at last began to be ordained in black churches. The first was Julia A.J. Foote who was ordained as a deacon in the AME Zion Church in 1884. However, it was not until nearly a hundred years later that a woman was

---

9. Jones: 24.
10. Andrews: 649.

ordained a minister; in 1976, Pauli Murray became the first African American female priest of the Episcopal Church at the National Cathedral of Washington, D.C.[11] Since that time, many women have joined Murray in leading African Americans in their quest for religious inspiration.

Griot (or griotte), historian, activist, revolutionary, spiritual leader, provider, crusader—the roles African American preachers, male and female, have played in the lives of their parishioners have been rich and varied, and have inspired generations. The messages and the very cadences of their sermons have influenced and been echoed in black poetry and prose, and even appeared in such non-religious compositions as modern rap music. Keeping the Faith is a sampling of this lyrical wealth of tradition and feeling. It is also a paean to the timelessness of the messages of freedom, equality, and liberation of the "keepers of the faith" included here, and an invitation to share the joys and woes, insights and inspiration of a group of men and women who were and are the bedrock of African American faith and culture.

Jim Haskins
Gainesville, FL
2002

---

11. Ibid.

Introduction

DR. MAYA ANGELOU

They Opened Their Hearts to the Lord.
They Opened Their Mouths to Anyone Who Would Listen.

The African American preacher, revered by many and reviled by some, can be credited with being the mainstay of a divergent, scattered, needful community. It is of more than passing interest to note that in 1792 when Richard Allen and Absalom Jones were refused ease in which to pray in a White segregated church, they walked out and began holding services for the free, newly free, and newly escaped slaves at the Freedman's Bureau in New York. Richard Allen, in his ministry, later established Mother Bethel AME Church in Philadelphia, Pennsylvania in 1822. Today in 2000, it represents among the oldest possession of land in the hands of African Americans. The African American preacher, during slavery, offered the only light in a grim and dreary time. Having taught himself to read despite the threat of lashings, beatings, and whippings, he took the scriptures and turned them into lyrics. He used poignant music, inspired by the affliction of slavery and the misery of want, and wrote the time defying Negro Spirituals. James Weldon Johnson wrote in 1910, "O black and unknown bards how came your lips to touch the sacred fire." Countee Cullen, another great African American poet wrote, "Yet do I marvel at this curious thing to make a poet Black and bid him sing." The successful African American preacher is a singing poet. He or she knows intimately the horror of poverty, the terror of powerlessness, and the dismaying of malignant neglect.

And yet, these African American preachers, in particular, stand out on faith that things will be better and offer to their listeners, to their parishioners, to the hopeless, the light of hope.

17

My mother's baby sister, after living "in the world," became a born again Christian in the Holiness Church. She studied the Bible and began to preach. She was known as Sister Leah and sometimes Reverend Leah. Her life was filled with good works, feeding the hungry, nursing the sick, and clothing the naked. She answered each telephone call by saying, "Praise the name of Jesus, Hello." When the query was, "Hello, how are you?" her response was, "Saved and Sanctified." My aunt prayed constantly aloud and sotto voce. She talked to Jesus as if he were her favorite big brother and to God as if he was literally her father or very close uncle.

That reminded me that African American preachers have an ease with God. They not only love God, they like God. And so, when they preach they speak as if God has just recently told them something and commanded them to relay the news to those in the church.

James Haskins has approached the majesty and mystery of the African American preacher with wonderful respect and appreciation. In this book, Keeping the Faith, the reader can hear the great drama that is enacted in the pulpit of the African American Church. In this book, we can nearly hear the melody the preacher composes as he speaks. Here, we find the soft voice telling us secrets made just for our ears and the bombastic voice meant to raise the dead (in church), to reach the hard of hearing, and to change the hardened heart. Haskins delivers a variety of homiletic offerings and we can choose our favorite.

As for me, I will have them all, for here, each preacher means to lift the heart up, to encourage our faith, and to really help us to build a brand new and better world for all.

Dr. Maya Angelou

A Question Out of the Darkness

GARDNER C. TAYLOR

During the twentieth century, Gardner C. Taylor followed in the footsteps of Absolom Jones in the fight for equality. During the 1960s, Taylor stood shoulder to shoulder with Martin Luther King Jr. in the battle for civil rights. Thirty years later, in the 1990s, he served as a counselor to Mayor David Dinkins, and he introduced Nelson Mandela to New Yorkers. Taylor served for forty-two years as pastor of the Concord Baptist Church in Brooklyn, New York.

In "A Question Out of the Darkness," Taylor turns to the Bible and the story of John the Baptist to give hope to those who face "the darkness and the cold." As with so many other sermons included here, Taylor's words give inspiration to all who seek to cry out against trouble.

A Question Out of the Darkness

And the disciples of John showed him of all these things. And John calling unto him two of his disciples sent them to Jesus, saying, Art thou he that should come? or look we for another? When the men were come unto him, they said, John [the] Baptist hath sent us unto thee, saying, Art thou he that should come? or look we for another? And in that same hour he cured many of their infirmities and plagues, and of evil spirits; and unto many that were blind he gave sight. Then Jesus answering said unto them, "Go your way, and tell John what things ye have seen and heard; how that the blind see, the lame walk, the lepers are cleansed, the deaf hear, the dead are raised, to the poor the gospel is preached." (Luke 7:18-22)

John the Baptist would have excited your imagination. First, there was the rugged, ascetic appearance and air of the man. His eyes were ablaze with a strange, intense fire, and his voice roared the judgment of God like peals of thunder, and his clothes were so different, exotic, strange, way out, actual camel's hair. Word drifted through the swank residential areas of Jerusalem that he ate the old diet of the desert, locusts and wild honey. This prophet, who held forth near the Jordan River, became the talk of the town. He was so picturesque, reminding the people of what they imagined the old prophets in Israel had been like. Some were deeply touched. Others were curious. But whatever the reason, one was not "not" in Jerusalem that season unless he had been out to the Jordan at least once to hear the preaching of John. People talked with a mixture of awe and respect and resentment of the things which this wilderness preacher was saying. His voice thundered about some impending judgment which hovered low and ominous like a cloud over the land. He talked about an "axe laid unto the root of the tree" and insisted that God was about to do some new and mighty things. People, well, their task was to prepare the way of the Lord and to make straight in the desert a highway upon which the new adventure of God might proceed. John would make you almost tremble as he raised again the lyrics of Isaiah, "Every valley shall be filled, and every mountain and hill shall be brought low, and the crooked shall be made straight, and the rough way shall be made smooth, and all flesh shall see the salvation of God."

There was that day, many would never forget it, when Jesus showed up among John's hearers. Something instantly softened and surrendered in the grim, unflinching spirit of the wilderness preacher. He saw, he believed, the answer! He saw in Jesus the very visitation of God. "Behold the lamb of God," he cried, "who taketh away the sins of the world." It was like the coming of springtime after a long and biting winter. Jesus was the answer. All would be well.

But then John ran afoul of the vengeance of cruel King Herod and was thrown into a dismal, unlighted cell. He was not in despair. Hadn't he seen Jesus and discovered in him God's visitation? Soon the deliverer would strike the blow that would bring the year of jubilee. Down the unlighted cell block, rushing feet would be heard racing, and the rusty doors would creak as they were thrown open to let John out into the sunlight again, a free man. Jesus would do it, only he didn't. Caged in his prison, it is hard to imagine the questions which began to plague the mind of John. Did Jesus know? He must have heard what happened. Why didn't he do something then?

At first he would smother the thought in his mind, ashamed of it. His plight, the silence of Jesus, long hours to brood, combined to make the question in John's mind too achingly sharp to be stifled any longer. "Hope deferred maketh the heart sick," wrote a wise man. And John's heart began to grow sick with doubt.

Is it that way with you? Heaven knows, you have tried to live a decent life, but things have turned out so poorly for you. You are imprisoned in ugly, terrifying conditions which you have done so little to deserve. Locked in sickness or imprisoned with family responsibilities which really belong to someone else, jailed by a dead end on the job, day after day you must get up to go through the old routine of quiet desperation. Night after night you stare into the darkness and stifle a sob and wonder deep down in your heart why God doesn't do something about it. If not so strapped, you and I ought to try to brace ourselves for those fearsome times when there is no light around us and the night of despair closes in upon us almost like choking fingers. A person can lose one's faith in the darkness if he or she is not careful and prayerful. Once I talked with a man by lovely Lake Geneva at the National Council of Churches assembly ground. He was a church executive, and in the gloaming he told me how in one year he lost his father, his wife, and his son. And then he said, "My grip nearly slipped." Sometimes in the darkness and the cold a person's grip will slip.

What is one to do then? What can one do? I like what John did as his grip of confidence in Jesus nearly slipped in the darkness of his prison cell. He did not conclude that all was hopeless and therefore there was no use attempting to do anything about the situation which wrenched his spirit and stuck in his heart like a dull, rusty sword. He decided to put the matter before the Master. John sent his friends to Jesus to report to him the anguished question which was tormenting the man in his prison cell. They sought an audience with Jesus and reported John's mood to him. "Our friend and former leader is in jail," they said. "His voice which once roared like thunder by Jordan's stream has been silenced by a vindictive king. He believed in you, and when you came to Jordan our teacher and leader, John, stepped out of the way saying that you, Jesus, must increase and he, John, must decrease. A long time now he has waited to hear in you footfalls of God's visitation to his people, Israel. He has believed that from you glorious tidings of deliverance would ring like stirring music through the land. But you have not been to see him, and you have not delivered him, and Israel still seems waiting for her redemption. Now, John has asked us to put the question to you bluntly. Art thou he that should come, the deliverer, the blessed of God? Or must we go back to the long, painful waiting for one who is come to set captive Israel free? Art thou he, or should we look for another?"

Jesus' answer is characteristic, for God will not be put on trial.

He is the judge of all the earth, and is not the defendant. He doe's not whine or beg. He states his case but does not wheedle or apple polish or grovel. God pleads, but always with the note of one who is in command. And so, Jesus sent a word back to the lonely, tormented prisoner which was neither yes nor no but which was far more. "Tell John what you have seen and heard. Tell John the blind see, the lame walk, the lepers are cleansed, the deaf hear, the dead are raised. To the poor the gospel is preached. Tell him to make his decision upon the basis of my record."

You and I may have cried out ever so desperately, only never to receive the answer we want. Look around now and you will see, I think, in your life signs that God is at work, though not as you requested. When we are ready to conclude that there is no God anywhere and hope is dead, we ought to consider how it has been with us in the past, through what difficulties we have somehow been led. If a soul must doubt God's goodness, let him first feel the warming sun on a cold and chilly day. If one must doubt God's providence and protection, let him first think of the dangers through which the soul has been led, as if by another hand. If a woman must doubt God's goodness and kindness, let her first remember the blessings that have been in her path and the ways that have opened before her. If a man doubt God's judgment, let him look first at history and see a steady, unyielding pressure upon people to fashion a fair world or suffer the guilt and turmoil of an unjust one. I think there is abundant evidence that there is a purpose and a mercy operating in your life and in the world. Do you remember the words of a well-loved steadying hymn,

> All the way my Savior leads me
> What have I to ask beside?
> Can I doubt His tender mercy,
> Who thru life has been my Guide?
> Heav'nly peace, divinest comfort,
> Here by faith in Him to dwell!
> For I know, whate'er befall me,
> Jesus doeth all things well.

The Words of Gardner Taylor

So to present to God whatever it is that troubles us and to cry out against it if need be, is our right as his people. Nor does it matter how bitter the complaint! Never forget the old psalm, "He knoweth our frame and remembereth that we are dust." There are days when we can bring before God a deep and glad laughter of joy and gratitude. There will be other days when we can only muster a bitter, angry complaint. If it is honest, be confident that God will accept whatever it is we truly have to lift up before him, and he will make it serve his purpose and our good.

The Sermon

C.C. LOVELACE

Using the metaphor of a train, "The Sermon" relentlessly catches us up and moves at breakneck speed along a path to a greater understanding of Jesus. The message of "The Sermon" and its use of call-and-response mix the zeal of the evangelist with the cadences of the griot of West Africa, bringing inspiration to listeners and readers alike.

The Sermon

A s heard by Zora by Zora Neale Hurston, at Eau Gallie in Florida, May 3, 1929

INTRODUCTION (spoken)

"Our theme this morning is the wounds of Jesus. When the Father shall ask, 'What are these wounds in throe hand?' He shall answer, 'Those are they with which I was wounded in the house of my friends.' (Zach. xiii. 6.)

"We read in the 53rd Chapter of Isaiah where He was wounded for our transgressions and bruised for our iniquities; and the apostle Peter affirms that His blood was spilt from before the foundation of the world.

"I have seen gamblers wounded. I have seen desperadoes wounded; thieves and robbers and every other kind of characters, law-breakers, and each one had a reason for his wounds. Some of them was unthoughtful, and some for being overbearing, some by the doctor's knife. But all wounds disfigure a person.

"Jesus was not unthoughtful. He was not overbearing. He was never a bully. He was never sick. He was never a criminal before the law and yet He was wounded. Now a man usually gets wounded in the midst of his enemies; but this man was wounded, says the text, in the house of His friends. It is not your enemies that harm you all the time. Watch that close friend. Every believer in Christ is considered His friend, and every sin we commit is a wound to Jesus. The blues we play in our homes is a club to beat up Jesus; and these social card parties . . ."

Before the hammers of creation
Fell upon the anvils of Time and hammered out the ribs of
the earth
Before He made ropes
By the breath of fire

And set the boundaries of the ocean by gravity of His power
When God said, ha!
Let us make man
And the elders upon the altar cried, ha!
If you make man, ha!
He will sin.
God my master, ha!
Christ, yo' friend said
Father!! Ha-aa!
I am the teeth of Time
That comprehended de dust of de earth
And weighed de hills in scales
Painted de rainbow dat marks de end of de departing storm
Measured de seas in de holler of my hand
Held de elements in an unbroken chain of controllment.
Make man, ha!
If he sin, I will redeem him
I'll break de chasm of hell

Where de fire's never quenched
I'll go into de grave
Where de worm never dies, Ah!
So God A'mighty, ha!
Got His stuff together
He dipped some water out of de mighty deep
He got Him a handful of dirt, ha!
From de foundation sills of de earth
He seized a thimble full of breath, ha!
From de drums of de wind, ha!
God my master!
Now I'm ready to make man

Aa-aah!
Who shall I make him after? Ha!
Worlds within worlds begin to wheel and roll

De Sun, Ah!
Gethered up de fiery skirts of her garments
And wheeled around de throne, Ah!
Saying, Ah, make man after me, Ah!
God gazed upon the sun
And sent her back to her blood-red socket
And shook His head, ha!
De Moon, Ha!
Grabbed up de reins of de tides
And dragged a thousand seas behind her
As she walked around de throne
Ah-h, please make man after me
But God said, No.
De stars bust out from their diamond sockets
And circled de glitterin throne cryin
A-aah! Make man after me

God said, No!
I'll make man in my own image, ha!
I'll put him in de garden
And Jesus said, ha!
And if he sin,
I'll go his bond before yo mighty throne
Ah, He was yo friend
He made us all, ha!

Delegates to de judgment convention
Ah!
Faith hasn't got any eyes, but she's long-legged
But take de spy-glass of Faith
And look into dat upper room
When you are alone to yourself
When yo' heart is burnt with fire, ha!
When de blood is lopin thru yo veins
Like de iron monasters (monsters) on de rail
Look into dat upper chamber, ha!
We notice at de supper table
As He gazed upon His friends, ha!
His eyes flowin wid tears, ha!
"My soul is exceedingly sorrowful unto death, ha!
For this night, ha!
One of you shall betray me, ha!
It were not a Roman officer, ha!
It were not a centurion soldier
But one of you
Who I have choosen my bosom friend
That sops in the dish with me shall betray me."
I want to draw a parable.
I see Jesus
Leaving heben with all of His grandeur

Disrobin Hisself of His matchless honor
Yieldin up de sceptre of revolvin worlds
Clothing Hisself in de garment of humanity
Coming into de world to rescue His friends.
Two thousand years have went by on their rusty ankles
But with the eye of faith I can see Him

Look down from His high towers of elevation
I can hear Him when He walks about the golden streets
I can hear 'em ring under his footsteps
Sol me-e-e, Sol do
Sol me-e-e, Sol do
I can see Him step out upon the rim bones of nothing
Crying I am de way
De truth and de light

God A'mighty!
I see Him grab de throttle
Of de well ordered train of mercy
I see kingdoms crush and crumble
Whilst de arc angels held de winds in de corner chambers
I see Him arrive on dis earth
And walk de streets thirty and three years
Oh-h-hhh!
I see Him walking beside de Sea of Galilee wid His disciples
This declaration gendered on His lips
"Let us go on the other side"
God A'mighty!
Dev entered de boat
Wid their oarus (oars) stuck in de back
Sails unfurled to de evenin breeze
And de ship was now sailin
As she reached de center of de lake

Jesus was 'sleep on a pillow in de rear of de boat
And de dynamic powers of nature become disturbed

And de mad winds broke de heads of de western drums
And fell down on de Lake of Galilee
And buried themselves behind de gallopin waves
And de white-caps marbilized themselves like an army
And walked out like soldiers goin to battle
And de ziz-zag lightning
Licked out her fiery tongue
Threw their wings in the channels of the deep
And bedded de waters like a road-plow
And faced de current of de chargin billows
And de terrific bolts of thunder-they bust in de clouds
And de ship begin to reel and rock
God A'mighty!
And one of de disciples called Jesus
"Master!! Carest thou not that we perish?"
And He arose
And de storm was in its pitch
And de lightnin played on His raiments as He stood
    on the prow of the boat
And placed His foot upon the neck of the storm
And spoke to the howlin winds
And de sea fell at His feet like a marble floor
And de thunders went back in their vault
Then He set down on de rim of de ship
And took de hooks of his power
And lifted de billows in His lap
And rocked de winds to sleep on His arm
And said, "Peace be still."
And de Bible says there was a calm.

I can see Him wid de eye of faith

When He went from Pilate's house
Wid the crown of 72 wounds upon His head
I can see Him as He mounted Calvary and hung upon de cross
    for our sins.

I can see-eee-ee
De mountains fall to their rocky knees when He cried
"My God, my God! Why hast thou forsaken me?"

And quickened de bones of de prophets
And they arose from their graves and walked about in de
streets of Jerusalem.
I heard de whistle of de damnation train
Dat pulled out from Garden of Eden loaded wid cargo goin to hell
Ran at break-neck speed all de way thru de law
All de way thru de prophetic age
All de way thru de reign of kings and judges
Plowed her way thru de Jordan
And on her way to Calvary when she blew for de switch
Jesus stood out on her track like a rough-backed mountain
And she threw her cow-catcher in His side and His blood
ditched de train,
He died for our sins.
Wounded in the house of His friends.
Thats where I got off de damnation train
And dats where you must get off, ha! For in dat mor-ornin', ha!
When we shall all be delegates, ha!
To dat judgement convention, ha!
When de two trains of Time shall meet on de trestle
And wreck de burning axles of de unformed ether

And de mountains shall skip like lambs
When Jesus shall place one foot on de neck of de sea, ha!
One foot on dry land
When His chariot wheels shall be running hub-deep in fire
He shall take His friends thru the open bosom of a unclouded sky
And place in their hands de hosanna fan
And they shall stand round and round His beatific throne
And praise His name forever.
Amen.

Lock-Jaw Lions:
Daniel in The Lions' Den

WYATT TEE WALKER

During the civil rights struggle of the 1960s, Wyatt Tee Walker served as Chief of Staff to Martin Luther King Jr. Since then he has achieved renown as a respected authority on African American religious music. The tale of "Daniel in the Lions' Den" has served to bolster the faith in God for centuries. In "Lock-Jaw Lions," Walker, senior pastor of the Canaan Baptist Church of Christ in New York City's Harlem community, makes a scholarly examination of the hymn based on this Biblical story, demonstrating both its appeal and its universal message of faith.

Lock-Jaw Lions:
Daniel in The Lions' Den

INTRODUCTION

This Prayer and Praise Hymn is set apart from all others so far as form is concerned. It is one of the rare "narrative" hymns that tell a complete Bible story as does Blessed Be The Name of the Lord in the first volume of this series. Daniel is even more unique because it has no apparent refrain. In this family of music, the refrain is the anchor of the hymn-poem. In performance, this writer has observed that Daniel is sung straight through without a return to the first stanza that usually serves as a refrain. This does not obtain in Daniel as illustrated on the lyric page. In all other hymns of this family of music, after all the stanzas have been sung or sometimes after each stanza is sung, a return to the first stanza (refrain) is made. The former prevails in most instances with the singing of the refrain to round off the singing of the music-piece. One must presume that after Angels locked the lions' jaws, there was no need to say anything else.

Curiously, the poetic form is one that has not been observed to date. The repetition resembles the "double basic" of the a a a b form but remains odd in this writer's experience with a three-line repeating lyric that has no variance in poetic form. This adds to the distinctiveness of this particular Prayer and Praise Hymn. Daniel arrests our attention on the additional ground that it describes one of the most spectacular and familiar occurrences in the Scriptures of God's rescue of a faithful servant

Daniel in the lions' den is one of the most beloved of Old Testament stories of the African American religious experience. It is no surprise then to find a Prayer and Praise Hymn based on this familiar narrative. In the chapter preceding, mention was made of the connection of this family of music to the Spirituals. That connection is again apparent since there is a well-known Spiritual entitled. Didn't My Lord Deliver Daniel which as the identical theme. The thematic similarity binds these two hymns together despite being created generations apart. It is further evidence, in some respect, of the continuity of theological thought of these Christians of African ancestry. In both eras the lesson of Daniel's deliverance from the den of lions was an expression of faith that their circumstance had not missed God's surveillance.

The Old Testament story of Daniel follows the overthrow of Belshazzar by Darius the Persian. Daniel had just deciphered the handwriting on the wall that predicted Belshazzar's doom and thus came well recommended to the Persian monarch. The empire was divided into one hundred and twenty provinces administered by three presidents of which Daniel was first. Daniel's favored position incurred the envy of the other presidents and princes of the one hundred and twenty provinces. By duplicitous means, they convinced Darius to issue a royal statute that prohibited prayer or petition to any "God or man for thirty days, save thee, O king . . ." The penalty for violation was to be cast into a den of lions. Daniel's enemies knew that he prayed three times a day without ceasing. Clearly aware of the king's edict, Daniel prayed as he always had. It is one of the earliest acts of civil disobedience on religious grounds.

In great haste, the presidents and kings informed the king that Daniel had broken the law and the lions' den rule must be invoked.

Despite the king's affection for the young Hebrew in exile, Darius was forced to have Daniel cast into the lions' den.

It is not difficult to fathom the reason for both the antebellum believers and those after the Civil War to grasp the hopefulness in Daniel's spectacular deliverance when one considers the hopelessness of their sociology. In both instances, the faith-response was that God delivered Daniel from the lions' den, so would He deliver his children of darker hue from the lions' den of slavery and twentieth century racism. Over and over again, the selection of Biblical sources for music material reflects the oppressed community's fascination with the extraordinary means of God's rescue of the faithful in the Scriptural record. The spiritual form of this Biblical theme includes a specific reference to Daniel's contemporaries, Hanania, Mishael and Azariah, more popularly known by their Babylonian names, Shadrach, Meshach and Abednego. During the reign of the Babylonian king, Nebuchadnezzar, they escaped the fiery furnace, again by spectacular means. The l'addition—the bottom line is that this hymn, as all others, posts its source of inspiration squarely in the Holy Bible.

THEOLOGICAL MOORING

Though the story of Daniel in the lions' den is specific in its context, it embraces a universal dictum: trust in God, as a Christian, is unequivocal. Earlier in his work, a reference was made to the "Job syndrome." The intention was to remind the reader that mature Christian faith must assume the Job stance: all the days of my appointed time will I wait, till my change come. Transliterated into our twentieth century jargon, Job's declaration means for the disciple of the Lord Jesus Christ, I will trust in the Lord until I die!

Daniel's response to the lions' den sentence is trust akin to Job's trust. Lions' den or no lions' den, Daniel would not compromise his faith in the God of Israel. The three Hebrew boys verbalized that faith in their resolute refusal to bow down to Nebuchadnezzar's idol of gold in the plain of Dura. They announced to the king that their refusal to bow down was based on their faith (in light of the fiery furnace sentence) that the God we serve is able to deliver us . . . In the same breath of conversation, they added, if he does not deliver us, be it known unto thee O king, that we will not serve thy gods, nor worship the golden image which thou has set up.

That sentiment must be at the heart of every devotee's commitment to God. Martin Luther's great hymn rings with that faith; the body they may kill, God's truth abideth still . . . His namesake Martin Luther King, Jr. repeatedly announced, if a man hasn't found something worth dying for, he isn't fit to live! It is the ultimate theology of the Cross. Calvary symbolizes the victory of defeat. The acid test of our personal faith is to determine that in the midst of hard trials and tribulation, whether we believe that God is able to deliver us and if He does not deliver us, will we trust Him anyway!

Our forbearers at the beginning of this century possessed a faith of that caliber. This Prayer and Praise Hymn is evidence that they trusted in the God of our salvation without any reservations. It is the bench-mark of Christian faith.

LYRIC AND FORM ANALYSIS

The poetic form of this hymn is unlike any other that has been encountered across the ten years of my focus on this music. In the hundreds of hymns examined, none possess the unwavering lyric style of Daniel in the Lions' Den. Oddly enough, the other stanzas remain just as rigid in form as the initial verses.

> Daniel in the lions' den (oh)
> Daniel in the lions' den (Lord)
> Daniel in the lions' den
> (Lions' den my Lord)
> Daniel in the lions' den (oh)

> Daniel in the lions' den (Lord)
> Daniel in the lions' den.

In the scheme above, I have inserted the interjections which aid in maintaining the pace of the hymn in a capella performance, the natural and historical style for this music. The insertions are a precise copy of the Bessie Jones' singers recorded as a part of the Southern Folk Heritage Series.

The hymn-tune is colloquial and is frequently used for other songs of this same genre. Its simplicity and familiar melody provide an easy vehicle for communal singing. It is, [of] course, repetitious, but varies slightly in the third and sixth line to give some small distinguishing character to the tune itself.

The progression of the stanzas follow in general form the thread of the story. There is no Biblical record of Daniel praying in the lions' den but the creators of this hymn knew he was a "praying man." With their "sanctified imagination" they provide the content of Daniel's "prayer" to God, viz, Lord have mercy on me and Now is a needy time. Given the circumstance (the lions' den), it is difficult to quarrel with their conclusions as to what might have been said. Daniel's assertion, You promise to answer prayer, is a product of the same assumptions about Daniel's prayer life. The last two stanzas are explicitly scriptural:

> The Daniel said unto the king.
> O king, live forever.
> My God hath sent his angel, and
> hath shut the lions' mouth . . .

There is a quaint beauty to this Prayer and Praise Hymn that is made unique because it has the rare form of telling a complete Bible story in song. The entire sixth chapter of Daniel is consumed with the details of this Old Testament narrative (28 verses). The genius of this hymn is that in very brief digest, the creators of this hymn have digested the core theology of what the Daniel/lions' den story is all about. It is surely another precious piece of our African American religious folklore.

CONTEMPORARY SIGNIFICANCE

In another published work that included a section on the African American Spiritual, I assigned to the spiritual form some observable characteristics. Among them was one, Eternality of message. That characteristic can as easily be assigned to this family of Black sacred music. Irrespective of the era in which this music first appeared and the precise details of the sociological context that prevailed, the message of this music remains timely.

The social circumstance of African Americans must be measured against the social circumstance of all other Americans. It is true that progress has been made so far as the race is concerned when compared to some other period in history. However, that progress is only relative. When compared to the progress of other Americans, the progress of Americans of African ancestry is negligible. If it is a given that our music is a mirror of our sociology, when it follows that the music created in another era remains relevant since there has been little consequential change in our fundamental sociology as compared to other Americans.

The message of Daniel essentially, deals with a circumstance of life that seems impossible to overcome. How can a mere man survive in a den of lions? But Daniel put his trust in God and was delivered in the lions' den. The indicia of African Americans' sociology is dismal, unpromising and bleak. Nixon, Reagan and Bush are cut from the same garment. We must do what Daniel did as this hymn details, place our complete trust in God for deliverance. He has the power to lock the lions' jaws!

Faith in a Foreign Land

JEREMIAH A. WRIGHT, JR.

While the cadences in C.C. Lovelace conjure the older rhythms of West Africa, Jeremiah A. Wright in "Faith in a Foreign Land" takes us there in the images drawn by his words, including a "meditation" written by Setiloane, a South African black man in the style of "African Praise Songs." The result is a powerful message of black pride, faith, and hope.

Faith in a Foreign Land

I want you to consider a familiar passage of Scripture as found in the Good News Bible (today's English Version).

> By the rivers of Babylon we sat down:
> there we wept when we remembered Zion.
> On the willows near by
> we hung up our harps.
> Those who captured us told us to sing:
> They told us to entertain them:
> "Sing us a song about Zion:"
> How can we sing a song to the LORD
> in a foreign land?"
>
> DANIEL 6:1-10

Come back with me in time, way back to a faraway place, and stand for a moment shoulder-to-shoulder with another people in another place, another time, and another predicament; a people in a predicament of pain nothing like yours, nothing like anything you've experienced or could even imagine. Just quietly stand and feel. Don't say a word; just let their lives speak to your life, their spirits to your spirit. Not even

47

a whisper, for they will fall strangely silent if they detect a stranger in their midst. Just stand where they stand for a moment and listen.

These are an African people, who for the most part are shepherds. They're a relatively peaceful people. They love music. Music permeates the fabric of their lives. They sing when a new life is conceived; they sing when a new baby is born; they sing while they work; they sing as they play. They do hand jive and hambone. They are famous for their rhyming and their rapping, and you ought to see and hear their little girls jump Double-Dutch. Such rhythms and made-up rhyming you've never heard.

They sing at weddings; they sing at funerals; some of them sing out their sermons; some of them sing out their prayers. They love music. Music permeates the fabric of their lives. They go into church saying, "Make a joyful noise unto the LORD all ye lands. Serve the LORD with gladness. Come before his presence with singing" (Psalm 100:1-2, KJV).

And drums? You ain't heard no drums until you hear this people on the drums. They have drums for church, drums for play; they have talking drums, male and female drums, and some drums you can hear in the summertime when the weather is warm, sort of beating the beat that makes even the deadbeats want to start moving. Music permeates every fabric of their lives.

And dance? You ain't seen no dancing. They just make up dancing on the spur of the moment, unchoreographed, unrehearsed. Music is like the air that surrounds every living thing for them. They are engulfed by music from the cradle to the grave. They make up impromptu songs to celebrate everything and anything—from a victory in battle, to a religious processional, to lovemaking between a man and a woman. These people love music and they love life. They love the deep things of life and the simple things of life, the things that give life meaning and the things that make life beautiful.

These are a profound people, a proud people, and a praying people. It was these people who built the pyramids, which our western minds, for all of their sophistication, still cannot figure out. It was these people who created the first cultures and developed the first civilizations on earth. It was these people, black of skin and wooly of hair, who gave to the world Pythagorean mathematics, and the cosmology of Thales of Miletus. It was these people, with their music and their rhythms who gave the world Epicurean materialism, Platonic idealism, Judaism, Christianity, and Islam. These are a profound people, a proud people, and a praying people.

A PEOPLE IN EXILE

But something has happened to these proud people. Stand here and listen. Let's see if we can learn what happened that makes them seem so different. Over here they're singing, and from the song they're singing, it sounds like they're in exile—snatched away from the homes they built, the places where they lived, and the sites that they loved; in exile—pulled away from their places of worship, where they met God and mysteriously felt God's awesome presence; in exile—taken away from the villages and towns where they grew up, fell in love, got married, settled down, started families, and began building on their dreams.

No longer are they in charge of their own lives; no longer are they in control of their daily activities; no longer are they able to sleep as husbands and wives, parents and children. And in some places no longer are they even considered to be human beings. Now they're looked upon as things, pieces of property, as "its," but never as "thous." They're toys to be played with, but never equals to be talked to; they're pieces to lie with, but never persons to be reckoned with or reconciled to; they're monkeys (if you listened to one racist guest who appeared on the "Oprah Winfrey Show"); they're nobodies, nothings, less than fully human, three-fifths of a person. In exile they are made fun of and mated like cattle. The song they sing sounds like a song sung from the bowels of exile. Listen to it:

Sometimes I feel like a motherless child, a long way from home.
In exile! Listen!
By the rivers of Babylon we sat down;
there we wept when we remembered Zion.
On the willows near by
we hung up our harps.

Those who loved music refused to sing in exile.
Those who captured us told us to sing:
They told us to entertain them.
"Sing us a song about Zion:"

In exile this pained people, 'buked and scorned, cried out,
How can we sing a song to the LORD
in a foreign land?

What has happened to this proud people is that they are in exile, and sometimes it's hard to make merry when you are being messed over and messed on. Wait a minute. Move away from the singing for just a moment and stand over here where the griot, the storyteller, is holding forth, weaving together a message with meaning, simultaneously giving us narration and interpretation. Listen to see if we can learn what happens to a people who are forced to live in a foreign land.

STRIPPED OF THEIR NAMES

The griot is talking about his ancestors, a man named Daniel and some friends of his who lived in exile. Early on in this tale (1:7), the griot tells us about one of the first things that happens to a people in exile. The chief official gave them new names: Belteshazzar, Shadrach, Meshach, and Abednego. The empire of today-those with brutal force, naked power, superior military might and, from time to time, those with somebody who is not wrapped too tight in the executive office; those who are drunk with power and mad with megalomania; the commander-in-chief of the imperial forces, the empire, strips the exiles of their names.

Daniel, Hananiah, Mishael, and Azariah, all of whom were from the tribe of Judah, were given new names by the empire. Daniel was given the name Belteshazzar. Hananiah was given the name Shadrach. Mishael was given the name Meshach, and Azariah was given the name Abednego. Centuries after the Bible story, people from the continent of Africa-places that today are the countries of Senegal, Guinea-Bissau, Gambia, Sierra Leone, Liberia, Cote D'Ivoire, Ghana, 'Ibgo, Benin, Nigeria, Cameroon, Equatorial Guinea, Gabon, Congo, Zaire, and Angola, were given new names by the empire: Negro, Negrito, Moreno, Prieta, Negress, Nigra, Nigger, Colored, Black, Coons, Sambo, Jungle Bunny, Boy, Girl, Uncle, and Mammy. The empire stripped the exiles of their names and imposed its own names upon them so that five or six generations later the original names were lost to memory except for the griot's, and the only names the exiles refer to are the names given by the empire.

When you take away a person's name, you take away his or her history. My name has a history to it; I did not choose it. It was selected for me by my ancestors, parents, and grandparents long before I was conscious of their decision and what went into that decision. My name has a history. I have a grandson. My son-in-law and my daughter selected my grandson's name long before that moment when we stood in that birthing room together and I got the shock of my life. In that birthing room the nurse said to my son-inlaw, "Have you picked out a name for your son?" And he turned around, grinned at me, and said, "His name is Jeremiah." My grandson's name has a history. Your name has a history, like John's name, Jesus' name, Samuel's name, and Daniel's name. They all have a history. They mean something. Daniel's name means "God is my judge." Samuel's

name means "ask of God" or "name of God." John means "Yahweh
has been gracious," and if you don't believe he has been gracious, ask
Zechariah and Elizabeth.

Hananiah also means "God has been gracious." Azariah means
"Yahweh has helped." Mishael means "Who is like God?" and Jesus
means "Yahweh is salvation." Names have a meaning; names have a
history. Wrapped up in a person's name is who he is, what family she
came from, and how God has blessed that particular family by his
grace in a particular manner.

No African would just willy-nilly change his or her name because
each name has a history to it. The Africans in North American chattel
slavery sang "I told Jesus it would be all right if he changed my name,"
but they didn't change their names, because wrapped up in their
names was their history. They sang "written down my name;" they
sang "Hush, somebody's calling my name;" they sang "I've got a new
name over in Glory, and it's mine, all mine." But no African ever willingly changed his or her own name, because that would be like telling
their mamas, their daddies, and their ancestors to go to hell, and
that's most uncharacteristic of Africans.

STRIPPED OF THEIR HISTORY

The North American slave owners, those "Babylonians," prototypes
of the empire and the imperialistic mind-set that disregards anything everybody else has ever done, did away with the natives' names
in an attempt to take away their history. As Chancellor Williams of
Howard University puts it in his question posed from a Sumer legend: "What became of the black people of Sumer?" the traveler
asked the old man (for ancient records show that the people of
Sumer were black). "What happened to them? Ah," the old man
sighed, "They lost their history, so they died." As Dr. Ofori Atta
Thomas of the Interdenominational Theological Center puts it,

"They forgot their story." They lost their history, so they died. Our children don't know our story. Any people who lose their story are a dead people. And the established authority, the empire, knows that, so it makes every deliberate attempt to take away the exiles' history. The empire tells them that they have no history prior to the Babylonians introducing them to civilization; the empire tells them outright lies and blatant distortions so that they will disown any linkage that they once had with Africa, and they become more Babylonian than the Babylonians.

If you downgrade where the exiles' came from and what they were once called, the grandchildren and great-grandchildren don't want to have anything to do with their history, and they embrace the culture of the "Babylonians." They walk around with Babylonian hairstyles, Babylonian clothes styles, Babylonian lifestyles, Babylonian ghetto blasters to their ears, and Babylonian cocaine monkeys on their backs. Yo, ya know what I'm sayin? We can out-Babylonian the Babylonians. In a foreign land, there is a deliberate attempt to take away the exiles' history and replace it with Babylonian history.

The Babylonians told the exiles such things as "In 592 Nebuchadnezzar sailed the ocean blue." (Ask the average African American child when Africans came to this country, and you get a blank stare. Ask them when Columbus discovered America. "Fourteen ninety-two." Columbus didn't discover America; he got lost in the Virgin Islands looking for India. The Indians discovered him.) Or the Babylonians told the exiles things such as: "In 586 when your ancestors were carried away into slavery, that was the best thing that ever happened to them, because through the goodness of the prejudiced Babylonian God, they were exposed to culture, literature, philosophy and fine arts, serious music and classical music." In a foreign land there is a deliberate attempt to take away an exile's history.

At our church during our seminarians' training, we looked at the tape that Dr. John Kinney, of Virginia Union University School of

Theology, did at the Hampton Ministers' Conference. He was telling us that that's how oppressors deal with marginalized people. The oppressors subsume them under a larger history, so that they can make the oppressed believe that they have never done anything. It's how some white folks trivialize black folks; they tell them that nothing they've done is important.

First they took their names so that they could take away their history—who they were and where they came from and how they got here. Listen to the griot as he tells Daniel's story. First (1:7), he tells how the empire took their names; then (1:4, 17) he tells us that Ashpenaz was to teach them to read and write in the Babylonian language. Verse 17 says God gave the four young men knowledge and skill in literature and philosophy. The empire stripped the exiles of their heritage. They were methodically taught how to read and write in the Babylonian language. Anyone who studies a foreign language knows that one of the first things you have to learn if you are going to learn the language fluently is how to think in that language. While you are learning to think in somebody else's language, your heritage is slowly taken away. For three years, 365 days a year, Daniel, Hananiah, Mishael, and Azariah were schooled and skilled in the knowledge of Babylonian literature and philosophy.

The African exiles who came to North America also were expected to learn the culture of their empire—their "Babylon." African Americans educated in this country have forgotten what their African forebears had created-the oral traditions and the written traditions. In fact, the "Babylonian" curriculum doesn't even include any African authors. There are just a token few "Afro-Babylonian" hybrids accepted into the canons. These exiles became schooled in Babylonian literature, from Beowulf to Virginia Wolfe, and their heritage was wickedly wiped away from the tissues of their memory banks. They became skilled in Babylonian philosophy from Descartes to Meister Eckhart, from Immanuel Kant to Jean Paul Sartre, from existentialism to nihilism, from the dialectical materialism of Karl Marx to the wissenschaftlichkeit of Martin Heidegger. They became skilled in Babylonian philosophy, and their heritage was demonically destroyed in the devious process.

Children of these African exiles are drilled in old Babylonian literature, middle Babylonian literature, Chaucerian Babylonian literature, Elizabethan Babylonian literature, Shakespearean Babylonian literature, seventeenth-century metaphysical Babylonian literature, eighteenth-century classical Babylonian literature, the nineteenth-century romantic Babylonian writers, and they do not know a thing about one of their writers, because after all, their writers never wrote what could be called serious or classical literature. Their heritage has been taken away from them.

From the African heritage, there are countless powerful writers. One of them, Gabriel Setiloane, who taught at the University of Capetown, is a pastor and a poet. You probably can't even go to some of our black colleges and universities to take a course where you can learn about Setiloane, a South African black man. I recommend one poem called "I Am an African."

This meditation is written in the characteristic style of "African Praise Songs" (Lithoko), which the Southern African recites before a Chief on important occasions. Sometimes a man will sing praises of himself also, telling of some strong personal experience, such as a battle, in former days, while today it might be about working in the mines or a long sojourn in a strange land.—G.S.

> They call me African;
> African indeed am I;
> Rugged son of the soil of Africa.
> Black as my father, and his before him:
> As my mother and sisters and brothers,
> living and gone from this world.

They ask me what I believe . . . my faith.
Some even think I have none
But live like the beasts of the field . . . .

"What of God, the Creator
Revealed to mankind through the Jews of old,
The YAHWEH: I AM
Who has been and ever shall be?
Do you acknowledge him?"

My fathers and theirs,
many generations before.
Knew him.
They bowed the knee to him
By many names they knew him.

And yet 'tis he the One and only God—
They called him:
UVELINGQAKI: The First One
Who came ere ever anything appeared;
UNKULUNKULU: The BIG BIG ONE,
So big indeed that no space could ever contain him:
MODIMO: Because his abode is far up in the sky.

They also knew him as MODIRI: For he has made all:
and LESFI: The spirit without which the breath of man
    cannot be.
But, my fathers, from the mouths of their fathers, say
That this God of old shone
With a brightness so bright
It blinded them . . . Therefore . . .
He hid himself. UVELINGQAKI,
That none should reach his presence . . .

Lest they die. (for pity flowed in his heart).
Only the fathers who are dead come into his presence,
Little gods bearing up the prayers and supplications
Of their children to the Great Great God . . .

That is one of the writings from the African heritage not included in almost any of the "Babylonian" curriculum—the curriculum that is accepted by the "establishment," the white educational system. In a foreign land there is the deliberate and devious attempt to take away the exile's heritage and replace it with a fabricated "Babylonian" heritage that distorts truths and tells outright lies. It is done so methodically and so thoroughly that after several generations you have African exiles paying homage to Hippocrates as the father of medicine, when clearly the African Imhotep discovered and practiced medicine centuries before Hippocrates was born. You have African exiles who know nothing at all about the Africans who were performing cataract surgery a thousand years before the birth of Hippocrates." You will have African exiles who think that unless the Babylonians said it, it ain't true; unless Babylonians wrote it, it ain't right; unless the Babylonians made it, it ain't gonna work.

THEY COULDN'T TAKE AWAY THEM FAITH

In a foreign land an identity crisis is created in a deliberate attempt to first take away the exiles' history and then to completely destroy the exiles' heritage. But as the griot continues to talk about what happens to folk in a foreign land, those forced to live there in exile, there is something else that he says about Daniel that causes his listeners to stir just a little bit. It seems as though the Babylonians went too far when they tried the ultimate thing that Babylonians try, and that is to take away an exile's religion. It seems as though they overstepped their bounds and did not understand how faith in a foreign land has a tenacity that defies description.

Let's let the griot tell his story. The griot says that Nebuchadnezzar's son, Belshazzar, had a banquet.' At his banquet he brought out sacred objects, which had been stolen from the temple in Jerusalem, and defiled them by pouring wine in those dedicated and consecrated bowls and cups. In the midst of his party a human hand from out of nowhere appeared and started writing on the wall. It wrote "mene, mene, tekel," and "parsin" (Daniel 5:25, RSV). And nobody could translate those words except Daniel, who interpreted it like this: "mene, God has numbered the days of your kingdom and brought it to an end; tekel, you have been weighed in the balances and found wanting; peres (singular of parsin), your kingdom is divided and given to the Medes and Persians" (5:26-28, RSV). That's what Daniel said, and that same night (it's something how the Lord works) Belshazzar, who desecrated those things taken from the temple, was killed; and Darius the Mede seized the royal power (as Daniel had said).

When Darius took office, he divided his empire into 120 provinces, and he put a governor in charge of each province. Over the governors he put three supervisors: Daniel and two others. And the supervisors only had one job: looking out after the king's interests. Daniel, like Joseph, rose from a position of nothing to a position of prominence in a foreign land, only Daniel did better. Daniel showed very quickly that exile or no exile, minority or culturally deprived, or any other label they wanted to pin on him, he could do better than all of the other supervisors and governors put together.

Daniel was sort of like a Doug Williams in a Super Bowl or a Martin King in the ministry or a'Ibni Morrison in the field of literature or a Ron McNair in the space program. He was like a Thurgood Marshall on the Supreme Court or a Michael Jordan or a Magic Johnson on the basketball court. He was like a Luther Vandross or a Stevie Wonder in the field of music or a Bo Jackson on the baseball and football fields. He was like a Jackie Joyner-Kersee on a track, or a Melanie Lawson on a news assignment in Panama."

He was like a Carl Lewis or an Edwin Moses in a foot race or like a Jesse Louis Jackson in a presidential race. Daniel could do better than all of them put together. And because he was so outstanding, the king considered putting him in charge of the whole empire (6:3), and that's when the "stuff" started. Those who are inferior can't stand those who are superior, especially when those who are superior are of a despised race, a race that everybody has been taught does not have the mental equipment to be superior. They tried their best to find something wrong with what Daniel was doing, but they couldn't, because he was honest and he was reliable.

So they said to one another, "We're not going to be able to pin anything on him unless it's in connection with this religion of his." You see, they had taken away his history and his name and had called him Belteshazzar. They had taken away his heritage and taught him Babylonian literature, language and philosophy. But when they tried the ultimate take-away —when they tried to take away his religion— they did what all oppressors do: they tried to take away his hope. But Daniel had the audacity to hope. When they tried to take away his hope, they found out that their trying was in vain.

First, they made up a lie and told the king, "Everybody, Your Honor, Your Majesty, all of us [that's a lie; they were including Daniel] including Daniel have come to this agreement . . . ." Then they told the king what their agreement was: "You ought to sign this order which says that nobody can ask anything of any man or any god for thirty days, and if they do, they'll be put in a pit." Then they got the king to sign the order and went to spy on Daniel to see what he was going to do. They knew that his religion was a way of life for him. They knew that he prayed to the God of his foreparents three times a day. They knew that come hell or high water, problems or protocol, this man of faith was a praying man, and he was going upstairs to his prayer room to throw open his windows toward Jerusalem and call upon the name of the Lord. They knew that morning, noon, and night-every day that the good Lord sent-this brother, whom they couldn't stand, was going to be down on his knees saying, "Thank you for another day. Thank you for another night's sleep. Thank you for being my God in a foreign land, just like you are my God in my homeland." They knew that decree or no decree, royal order or no royal order, this man who believed in the power of prayer, this man whose hope was in the Holy One of Israel, would be in that window, hollering, "Father, I stretch my hands to thee. No other help I know."

So they ran as soon as the order was signed to see what God's servant would do. But, verse 10 says they could not take away his hope. When Daniel learned that the order had been signed, he went home and there, just as he had always done, Daniel knelt down at that open window and prayed. You don't pray based upon what a king says; you pray based upon your relationship with the King of kings. Whenever you feel like calling on him, you call on him; you pray. Not when the "empire" says pray. You pray every time you feel the spirit moving in your heart.

When Daniel knelt down and prayed to God, maybe he called him Yahweh; maybe he called him Joshua, "Yahweh is salvation;" maybe he called him Miqveh, "the one hope, upon whom Israel is waiting;" maybe he called him Uvelingqaki, "the first one who came e'er anything appeared. Maybe he called him

Unkulunkulu, "so high you can't get over him, so low, you can t get under him, so wide you can't get around him;" maybe he called him Modimo, whose abode "is far up in the sky." Maybe he called him Modiri, "for he has made all." Maybe he called him Lesa, the rush, the pneuma, the breath of God without which we could not live. Maybe he called him the God of Abraham and Sarah. Maybe he called him Mary's Baby or Gehazi s Judge." Maybe he called him what my grandparents used to call him: Rock in a weary land, Shelter in the time of storm.

Maybe he called him Joshua's Battleaxe, Jeremiah's Fire, or Ezekiel's Wheel. But whatever he called him, the message was the same to that listening community, and that message still is, "Hold onto your faith, even in a foreign land. Hold onto the hope that is within you, the hope that maketh not ashamed. Hold onto God's unchanging hand, no matter how hard the circumstances are around you or how they may change." Say like Daniel, and like the African said in slavery, "Yes, there is trouble all over this world, but I ain't gonna lay my 'ligion down."

Folks may mess with your history and make it hard for you to uncover it. They may mess with your heritage and cause you to forever see yourself through the tainted lenses of somebody else, but don't let go of your hope. Hold on to the faith that your mama had; hold on to the faith that your daddy had. Your faith will give you transporting power. It will carry you through dark days and lonely nights. It will give you transcending power by which you will rise above the muck and mire all around you. It will give you transforming power that will change not only you, but those around you, too. Hold on to your faith, even in a foreign land.

Don't let go of the hope that sustains you, no matter how dark the night, no matter how steep the mountain, no matter how deep the valley. Don't let go of the hope that Dr. Watts calls our hope for years to come. No matter how difficult the circumstances, no matter how vicious the enemy, don't let go of your hope. Get up in the morning saying, "My hope is built on nothing less than Jesus' blood and righteousness." Go to bed at night saying, "I dare not trust the sweetest frame, but wholly lean on Jesus' name." Don't let go of your hope, no matter how high up you go on the "Babylonian" ladder.

You see, some of us have been taught this thing all wrong by some "Babylonians." They taught a lot of us that the higher up you go, the more soft and sophisticated you are supposed to become. We get one or two degrees from the "Babylonian" educational system, and we get "right cultured" and "right quiet." We're too sophisticated to say, "Thank you, Jesus." We're too assimilated to wave our hands. We're too acculturated to praise God anyhow. I know what I'm talking about because I have been there.

But Daniel, who had gone all the way up the ladder as high as he could, threw open his windows and hollered out as loudly as he could. You see, the higher up you go, the louder you're supposed to holler. Don't get too proud to praise the Lord. Hold on to your faith. You can become a dean or a president, head or CEO of a corporation, but don't let go of a balm in Gilead.

There was a time when I didn't understand this. My mama used to be an embarrassment to me. My mama finished college at an earlier age than Martin Luther King finished. She had a master's degree at eighteen and a second master's at twenty-one. She earned a Ph.D. from the University of Pennsylvania, and my mama, with all of that education, would say every time somebody preached or prayed, "Well! Well! Well!" See the "Babylonians" taught me you were supposed to be laid back and cool; you don't make comments when someone's preaching. That's how I used to be. Oh, but when God touched my life . . .

When I graduated from Howard University, I was still up under that "Babylonian" weight, so I looked around to see who was watching me, and I said a cool, "Thank you, Jesus." When they gave me my master's degree, I was a little higher up and felt a little more free, so I said a little louder, "Thank you, Jesus." People were looking at me. Then, when it was time for my doctorate, the president of the university was there; the chancellor was there. They put the diploma in my hand and said, "All the rights and privileges there unto appertaining," and I said, "Thank you, Jesus!" The higher up you go, the louder you're supposed to holler. Don't let go of your faith, even in a foreign land.

If you want to know how to hold on, no matter what, just remember the story of my daddy. My daddy used to be an embarrassment to me until I found out a few things. He came straight off the farm. His father sent him to college with twenty-five cents, and Daddy had twelve earned letters behind his name: a B.Th., a B.A., an M.Div., and an S.T.M. He had four degrees: one undergraduate, two graduate from Virginia Union University, a black school, and one from the Lutheran School of Theology. Like Martin Luther King, my daddy's mind had been honed by the finest scholarship in German theological circles. Like Daniel, my daddy knew "Babylonian" theology, christology, homiletics, and hermeneutics. He had studied "Babylonian" exegesis and mastered form criticism.

My daddy had gone all the way up the ladder, but where the "Babylonians" had honed his mind, the God of Abraham and Sarah had tuned his heart. When he came home from his ministerial association meeting one cold Monday afternoon in September of 1941, they told him that his wife, who had had a difficult pregnancy, had passed out on the floor. The baby had come out six months into her pregnancy with the umbilical cord wrapped around its neck. At the hospital the baby had been pronounced dead on arrival, and they were trying to save his wife. My daddy didn't call on no "Babylonian" theology; my daddy didn't look up no "Babylonian" christology; my daddy got down on his knees right there on the floor next to his wife's blood and called on the God of Abraham and Sarah, Isaac and Rebekah, and said, "Lord, if you can and if you will, I know you can save my boy." And fifty-two years later, here is the one that was pronounced dead on arrival. Don't you till me what God can't do. God stepped into that emergency room. While my father was just praying, the Lord stepped in and changed the diagnosis from dead on arrival to divinity on the agenda.

Thank God! Thank God! Don't let go of your faith. I don't care how high up you go. Don't let go of your faith.

Holding on to Your Song

W. FRANKLYN RICHARDSON II

The Rodney King beating and trial in Los Angeles in the 1990s created a climate of anger, "anxiety and anguish" within black communities. In "Holding On To Your Song," W. Franklyn Richardson urges those confronted by these destructive emotions not to give way to them, to remember tradition, to recall Jesus, and to pray for joy in the face of adversity. Richardson's message transcends the moment, giving solace to all facing tribulation, not merely those facing the trials to which he alludes.

Holding on to Your Song

This week's activity in our nation and in Los Angeles has been on all of our lips and in all of our thinking and in our reflection. The incident with Rodney King in Los Angeles and the aftermath of it, the response by our community, in Los Angeles and around the nation have served to provide the background and the impact of the sermonic decision for this morning.

It is with that on my heart and mind that I want to solicit your attention to one of the great psalms of our tradition. It is the psalm that captures to some degree the kind of anxiety and anguish that we feel in our nation. It is in that 137th psalm and I want to read this morning the fourth verse, How shall we sing the Lord's song in a strange land. The Hebrews for whom these words reflect the time of their reflection have been in bondage, captivity by the Chaldeans. They had been persecuted. They had been robbed of their homeland. Taken to a new hostile nation. Robbed of their culture and customs. Made to be servants under the rule and reign of the Chaldeans and at the time of our text the writer says that the text in question and query is really a response to the request made by the captors, the oppressors of the Hebrews. The request made was we want you to be happy. We want you to entertain us. We want you to be joyful. We want you to sing us some of the songs of your tradition. We want you to sing for our amusement.

The Scripture says that when they made that request these Hebrews who were in a hostile and terrified land answered how shall we sing the Lord's song in a strange land. There is a sense in which the land in which we as African Americans live in this nation is a hostile land. There is a sense in which we are an oppressed people. There is a sense in which we are victims of systemic racism and mean and cruel people, some of whom don't even know that they are responding to racist signals, use their time and their energies to hold and crush a whole nation of people down.

It's a hostile land. Our young boys and girls are on crack and cocaine and heroin and other drugs at a disproportionate number to our percentage of the population. Our young men are in jail in disproportionate numbers to the nation. One out of every four, 25 percent of all Black men in this nation are related to the penal system one way or another. It's a hostile land for us. In Los Angeles just before the riots and Rodney King, 50 percent of Black men in that city were unemployed. Two out of every four men, Black men had no job and nowhere to look for a job, and no signal of sensitivity coming from the White House or the state house or the council chambers. It's a hostile land. When you look at the alarming statistics that tell of the quality of life of African Americans in the nation we live in a hostile situation.

However, we must be careful. We must search for the question that was raised by the Hebrews in our text. We must ask the question in spite of all that we are going through, in spite of all the pain and all of the oppression and all the racism that shows up everywhere we look we must ask ourselves the question how can I hold on to my music and not lose my song in a strange land. We have to ask ourselves the question how can I still keep believing, how can I still keep going on in spite of how bad things are. We must ask ourselves the question this morning how shall we sing the Lord's song. When one looks at the statistics of AIDS in our communities as compared to AIDS in other communities, not only AIDS but cancer when one gathers the statistics that a Black man has a better chance of surviving in one of the poorest nations in the world, India, than he does in Harlem, we are in a hostile situation, but somehow we've got to find the answer to the question how can we still hold on to our music, how can we still not be overcome, how can we avoid being an accomplice to our own sense of frustration and become victims at our own hands how can we keep our music.

It's important, you know, to be able to have music in your life that transcends context and circumstance. You've got to somehow have the ability to rise above what you're going through. There's no short answer, there's no short cut, but if we are going to survive, if we are going to make it, we've got to have the capacity to rise above our circumstance and be all that we can be.

Benjamin Mays once said that he got on the bus, president of the university, back in the 50s, said he got on the bus and the bus driver told him to get to the back of the bus. Told him to take his place, so, one of the college students came and he said, Dr. Mays do you mean you gonna let a bus driver—you are a president of a university, have all that education—and you gonna let a bus driver insult you. He said, young man the bus driver can't insult me. He said, he told me to sit in the back of the bus and the only way that I was able to sit there, my mind never got in the back of the bus, my body was in the back of the bus and I knew that one day my body would join my mind in the front of the bus.

Somehow we must have the capacity to rise above whatever context we find ourselves and hold on to the joyful triumph, the sounding notes of hope and possibility in the midst of all of the hostilities to which we pass. How can we sing the Lord's song in a strange land. I want to submit to you this morning that these Hebrews they may have somehow found the twist for it. If they had sat long enough and prayed long enough somehow one can come to know that I can have music in my life. Music is symbolic of purpose and meaning.

How do you hold on to your purpose? How do you hold on to your joy? How do you hold on to the quality of life in your journey when everything around you is pulling you down and denying your personhood? The first thing that we have to do is to understand that we must never allow our location and our situation to obscure our destination. We must never allow, no matter how bad things get, no matter how mean the folk get, we must not ever allow them, like Benjamin Mays, to help us to obscure the fact that we have a more noble destination to which we are moving and we cannot allow temporary and present frustration cause us to fail to understand where we are. You and I must not allow it. In our own individual lives, not matter what you are passing through here this morning you've got to always understand that whatever you are going through, it is that you are going through it, you have not come to it. You have not come to the end of the road no matter what's going on in your life.

People who commit suicide are those who fail to understand the perspective of their troubles. They think that the trouble is the end to which they have come and they have not understood that they have not come to an end, they are just passing through on their way to a distant designation. Don't ever let your troubles get so bad, don't ever let your circumstance become so depressing that you lose perspective on what's happening in your life. I don't care how bad things are, don't care how much trouble is in your home, how much trouble is with your children, how much trouble is on your job or in the society, don't care how much sickness you have in your body don't allow whatever you are going through to fool you and make it look like it's what you've come to, it is just something through which you are passing.

Our forefathers and mothers knew that. John Malcolm Ellison, in his book "They Sang Through a Crisis" said very eloquently and profoundly that our forefathers and mothers, even though they experienced a kind of hardship, a kind of victimization, a kind of slavery that you and I knew nothing about and know nothing about, as bad as things are it's not as bad as they were and somehow they held on to their perspective. They held on to a sense of understanding that nobody would steal their song. And when the storm got heavy, when the clouds seem to roll over their heads, I'm so glad they left us the perspective in their language of their music. They said this about the storm when they saw the storms in their lives, and you know if you live you gonna have some storms, you'll have storms in your house, in your job, with your children, with your spouses, with your career, storms are all around, but our forefathers and mothers looked up at the storm and they did not focus on the storm, they focused on the movement of the storm and they said the storm is passing over—hallelujah.

The hallelujah was not intended to celebrate the fact that the storm was there but to celebrate the perspective of the storm. That the storm is passing by and if you've got some storms in your life this morning just hold on, get the right perspective. Hold on because I read in my Bible that when you are too tired to fight, when you can't go on any further, when you've used up all of your energy, stand still and they that wait upon the Lord shall renew their strength. They shall mount up on wings like eagles.

Somehow, somehow we must never allow our location and our situation to obscure our destination. We can't let a decision in a courtroom that goes against justice, we can't let a mean, insensitive man who sits in a White House or in a state house or in a council chamber to cause us to lose perspective on our destination. We've got a better way and a better place and ultimately we will be all that God wants us to be.

Then secondly, I want to submit to you that one of the ways that you can hold on to your music and not allow anything and anybody to steal your song is not to become focused on the people who are doing you in. This text is not a real Christian text, it's in the Bible but it ain't Christian. The closing of the psalm—when you go home, read it, they make some rather un-Christian statements. These Hebrews say of the Chaldeans, they say we hope that what you did to us somebody does to you. They say down in that text, they said we hope that somebody will come along and take your children and throw them up against the stones like you threw our children up against the stone. Well, my brothers and sisters, whenever you focus on somebody who's done you in, and this may be hard to swallow, but whenever you focus on getting back at somebody who's treated you wrong or mistreated you in your life, or held you down, or been a stumbling block, it will rob you of your music, it will take the joy out of your life. There is a sense in which hatred robs us of our perspective. You can go along all you want to and if you spend your life hating the folk who have been doing you wrong it will do more to destroy you than it will ever do to destroy the folk who did you wrong.

Somehow we as a people can never focus our energies on the people who did us in. We don't have time to go around hating white folks. We've got to go around loving ourselves too much that we ain't got time to hate anybody who's done us wrong because when we go around hating folk who have done us wrong we become an accomplice to our own oppression. We become participants in our own destruction. We become vehicles to destroy our own community. Somehow we've got to believe that God is right when He said: "Vengeance is Mine sayeth the Lord." Don't you worry about getting back. You get on with the business of kingdom building. You get on with the business of nation building. You get on with the business of being all that God wants you to be and the Lord will take care of the rest because my Bible teaches you gotta reap what you sow. Whatsoever goes around comes around and sooner or later you will pay for what you do. You cannot go through life hating folk. Life is too short. It will rob you of your joy. It's too short. The days are not enough. The nights come too fast and the next thing you know it's over and you'll spend up all your energy carrying burdens of hatred.

Early on in my life, when I first got married 22 years ago, I'd get mad at my wife and stay mad two or three days until one day I realized that she wasn't paying me no mind. I was going around mad, my mouth poked out and she was going on singing and being happy. And the hatred was doing me in, robbing me of my joy and she was going on singing and still enjoying life and I wasn't going to do nothing but make myself miserable and that's the way a whole lot of us are, we carry that hatred around in our hearts, it doesn't do anything to the person you hating, but it's slowly destroying your own sense of joy and purpose and taking the smile off your face and leaving you bitter and finding that there's no joy. You and I we cannot afford it. It's too expensive. It costs too much. Hatred is too expensive to carry. Hatred causes Cancer. Hatred causes diseases. Hatred flourishes in high blood pressure. It destroys the holder, the possessor and not the object of the hate. So, you and I must somehow be able to free ourselves, be therapeutic enough to unload ourselves of hatred and get on with the business of doing what it is that God's got for us to do. I got too short to live. My days are too short to spend in hating you and so you and I got to go through life and not allow anybody to steal the music out of our lives.

One of the great assets of us as a people is that we've been able to sing through the crisis. We've been able to not allow, as bad as things have been, we've somehow been able to hold on to our song. We are some of the most happiest people to have gone through the worst circumstances that you'll ever see and we can't allow anybody to steal our song. Not only collectively, but individually. Don't you allow anybody to take the music out of your life. Don't you allow a mean husband, a mean wife, unruly children, an uncaring community, an insensitive leader, don't you let nobody steal the joy out of your life. Don't let nobody stop you from seeing the celebration in the sunrise or the beauty in a rose or the purity of a lily or the breaking of a butterfly or the setting of a hill or the flowing of a stream, don't let nobody take your song, steal the music. Steal the music out of your life. Not gonna let anybody steal my music, steal my joy.

Folk who don't know Jesus, they don't know how we can do it. They say how you do that, how you all can sing when folk messing with you, how you all keep on smiling when folk putting you down, how is it that you keep on feeling good when everything around you ought to make you feel bad, how is it Christian that you can be happy with cancer and high blood pressure and children that won't do right, how is it Christian that you can keep on singing? Well, we got an answer for them: I sing, Oh I sing because I'm happy, I sing because I'm free, His eye is on the sparrow, now if He watching over the sparrow you know He's watching over me. I sing because I'm happy, I sing because I'm free, ain't gonna let nobody steal my song. Turn to somebody and tell them: I ain't gonna let nobody steal my song. The doors of the church open. Somebody here ought to join the church. Come on now don't let nobody steal your song.

A Thanksgiving Sermon

ABSALOM JONES

During the summer of 1792, the Methodists of St. George's Methodist Church in Philadelphia completed the building of a gallery in which black members of the church were told to sit. During one service, Richard Allen and Absolom Jones and other black members of the congregation were told to move to the rear of the gallery. In protest, as Allen later said, "All went out of the church in a body and they were no more plagued with us in the church." The result of this protest was the formation of two new churches for black church goers, one of which—St. Thomas Episcopal Church, founded in 1794—was led by Absolom Jones. In 1795, Absolom Jones was ordained as the first black Episcopal priest in the United States.

Jones rose to prominence not only for his work against inequality, but also for his forceful oratory. "A Thanksgiving Sermon" is a call for an annual day of thanksgiving to be held each January 1st, the day that an act was passed by the United States Congress barring the African slave trade. It is also the emotional expression of gratitude to the God who oversaw this act and those who carried it out. Although given in 1808, the emotion behind this sermon is as moving today as when it was heard by Jones's thankful congregation.

A Thanksgiving Sermon

Preached January 1, 1808, in St. Thomas's, or the African Episcopal, Church, Philadelphia: On Account of The Abolition of the African Slave Trade, On That Day, by the Congress of the United States

> And the Lord said, I have surely seen the affliction
> of my people which are in Egypt, and have heard
> their sorrows; and I am come down to deliver them
> out of the hand of the Egyptians.
>
> EXODUS III, 7-8

These words, my brethren, contain a short account of some of the circumstances which preceded the deliverance of the children of Israel from their captivity and bondage in Egypt.

They mention, in the first place, their affliction. This consisted in their privation of liberty: they were slaves to the kings of Egypt, in common with their other subjects; and they were slaves to their fellow slaves. They were compelled to work in the open air, in one of the hottest climates in the world: and, probably, without a covering from the burning rays of the sun. Their work was of a laborious kind:

it consisted of making bricks, and travelling, perhaps to a great distance, for the straw, or stubble, that was a component part of them. Their work was dealt out to them in tasks, and performed under the eye of vigilant and rigorous masters, who constantly upbraided them with idleness. The least deficiency, in the product of their labour, was punished by beating. Nor was this all. Their food was of the cheapest kind, and contained but little nourishment: it consisted only of leeks and onions, which grew almost spontaneously in the land of Egypt. Painful and distressing as these sufferings were, they constituted the smallest part of their misery. While the fields resounded with their cries in the day, their buts and hamlets were vocal at night with their lamentations over their sons; who were dragged from the arms of their mothers, and put to death by drowning, in order to prevent such an increase in their population, as to endanger the safety of the state by an insurrection. In this condition, thus degraded and oppressed, they passed nearly four hundred years. Ah! Who can conceive of the measure of their sufferings, during that time? What tongue, or pen, can compute the number of their sorrows? To them no morning or evening sun ever disclosed a single charm: to them, the beauties of spring, and the plenty of autumn had no attractions: even domestick endearments were scarcely known to them: all was misery; all was grief; all was despair.

Our text mentions, in the second place, that, in this situation, they were not forgotten by the God of their fathers, and the Father of the human race. Though, for wise reasons, he delayed to appear in their behalf for several hundred years; yet he was not indifferent to their sufferings. Our text tells us, that he saw their affliction, and heard their cry: his eye and his ear were constantly open to their complaint: every tear they shed, was preserved, and every groan they uttered, was recorded; in order to testify, at a future day, against the authors of their oppressions. But our text goes further: it describes the Judge of the world to be so much moved, with what he saw and what he heard, that he rises from his throne—not to issue a command to the armies of angels that surrounded him to fly to the relief of his suffering children—but to come down from heaven, in his own person, in order to deliver them out of the hands of the Egyptians. Glory to God for this precious record of his power and goodness: let all the nations of the earth praise him. Clouds and darkness are round about him, but righteousness and judgment are the habitation of his throne. O sing unto the Lord a clew song, for he bath done marvelous things: his right hand and his holy arm hath gotten him the victory. He hath remembered his mercy amid truth toward the house of Israel, and all the ends of the earth shall see the salvation of God.

The history of the world shows us, that the deliverance of the children of Israel from their bondage, is not the only instance, in which it has pleased God to appear in behalf of oppressed and distressed nations, as the deliverer of the innocent, and of those who call upon his name. He is as unchangeable in his nature and character, as he is in his wisdom and power. The great and blessed event, which we have this day met to celebrate, is a striking proof, that the God of heaven and earth is the same, yesterday, and to-day, arid for ever. Yes, my brethren, the nations from which most of us have descended, and the country in which some of us were born, have been visited by the tender mercy of the Common Father of the human race. He has seen the affliction of our countrymcn, with an eye of pity. He has seen the wicked arts, by which wars have been fomented among the different tribes of the Africans, in order to procure captives, for the purpose of selling them for slaves. He has seen ships fitted out from different ports in Europe and America, and freighted with trinkets to be exchanged for the bodies and souls of men. He has seen the anguish which has taken place, when parents have been torn from their children, and children from their parents, and conveyed, with their hands and feet bound in fetters, on board of ships prepared to receive them. He has seen them thrust in crowds into the holds of those ships, where many of them have perished from the want of air. He has seen such of them as have escaped from that noxious place of confinement, leap into the ocean, with a faint hope of swimming back to their native shore, or a determination to seek an early retreat from their impending misery, in a watery grave. He has seen them exposed for sale, like horses and cattle, upon the wharves, or, like bales of goods, in warehouses of West India and American sea ports. He has seen the pangs of separation between members of the same family. He has seen them driven into the sugar, the rice, and the tobacco fields, and compelled to work—in spite of the habits of ease which they derived from the natural fertility of their own country— in the open air, beneath a burning sun, with scarcely as much clothing upon them as modesty required:

He has seen them faint beneath the pressure of their labors. He has seen them return to their smoky huts in the evening, with nothing to satisfy their hunger but a scanty allowance of roots; and these, cultivated for themselves, on that day only, which God ordained as a day of rest for man and beast. He has seen the neglect with which their masters have treated their immortal souls; not only in withholding religious instruction from them, but, in some instances, depriving them of access to the means of obtaining it. He has seen all the different modes of torture, by means of the whip, the screw, the pincers, and the red hot iron, which have been exercised upon their bodies, by inhuman overseers: overseers, did I say? Yes: but not by these only. Our God has seen masters and mistresses, educated in fashionable life, sometimes take the instruments of torture into their own hands, and, deaf to the cries and shrieks of their agonizing slaves, exceed even their overseers in cruelty. Inhuman wretches! though You have been deaf to their cries and shrieks, they have been heard in Heaven. The ears of Jehovah have been constantly open to them: He has heard the prayers that have ascended from the hearts of his people; and he has, as in the case of his ancient and chosen people the Jews, come down to deliver our suffering countrymen from the hands of their oppressors. He came down into the United States, when they declared, in the constitution which they framed in 1788, that the trade in our African fellow-men, should cease in the year 1808: He came down into the British Parliament, when they passed a law to put an end to the same iniquitous trade in May, 1807. He came down into the Congress of the United States, the last winter, when they passed a similar law, the operation of which commences on this happy day. Dear land of our ancestors! thou shall no more be stained with the blood of thy children, shed by British and American hands: the ocean shall no more afford a refuge to their bodies, from impending slavery: nor shall the shores of the British West India islands, and of the United States, any more witness the anguish of families, parted for ever by a public sale. For this signal interposition of the God of mercies, in behalf of our brethren, it becomes us this day to offer up our united thanks. Let the song of angels, which was first heard in the air at the birth of our Saviour, be heard this day in our assembly: Glory to Cod in the highest, for these first fruits of peace upon earth, and good-will to man: O! let us give thanks unto the Lord: let us call upon his name, and make known his deeds among the people. Let us sing psalms unto him and talk of all his wondrous works. Having enumerated the mercies of God to our people, it becomes us to ask, What shall we render unto the Lord for them: Sacrifices and burnt offerings are no longer pleasing to him: the pomp of public worship, and the ceremonies of a festive day, will find no acceptance with him, unless they are accompanied with actions that correspond with them. The duties which are inculcated upon us, by the event we are now celebrating, divide themselves into five heads. In the first place, Let not our expressions of gratitude to God for his late goodness and mercy to our countrymen, be confined to this day, nor to this house: let us carry grateful hearts with us to our places of abode, and to our daily occupations; and let praise and thanksgivings ascend daily to the throne of grace, in our families, and in our closets, for what God has done for our African brethren. Let us not forget to praise him for his mercies to such of our colour as are inhabitants of this coun-try; particularly, for disposing the hearts of the rulers of many of the states to pass laws for the abolition of slavery; for the number and zeal of the friends he has raised up to plead our cause; and for the privileges we enjoy, of worshiping God, agreeably to our consciences, in churches of our own. This comely building, erected chiefly by the generosity of our friends, is a monument of God's goodness to us, and calls for our gratitude with all the other blessings that have been mentioned.

Secondly, Let us unite, with our thanksgiving prayer to Almighty God, for the completion of his begun goodness to our brethren in Africa. Let us beseech him to extend to all the nations in Europe, the same humane and just spirit towards them, which he has imparted to the British and American nations. Let us, further, implore the influence of his divine and holy Spirit, to dispose the hearts of our legislatures to pass laws, to ameliorate the condition of our brethren who are still in bondage; also, to dispose their masters to treat them with kindness and humanity; and, above all things, to favour them with the means of acquiring such parts of human knowledge, as will enable them to read the holy scriptures, and understand the doctrines of the Christian religion, whereby they may become, even while they are the slaves of men, the freemen of the Lord.

Thirdly, Let us conduct ourselves in such a manner as to furnish no cause of regret to the deliverers of our nation, for their kindness to us. Let us constantly remember the rock whence we mere heron, and the pit whence roe mere dinged. Pride was not made for man, in any situation; and, still less, for persons who have recently emerged from bondage. The Jews, after they entered the promised land, were commanded, when they offered sacrifices to the Lord, never to forget their humble origin; and hence, part of the worship that accompanied their sacrifices consisted in acknowledging, that a Syrian, ready to perish, was their father. in like manner, it becomes us, publicly and privately, to acknowledge, that an African slave, ready to perish, was our father or our grandfather. Let our conduct be regulated by the precepts of the gospel; let us be sober minded, humble, peaceable, temperate in our meats and drinks, frugal in our apparel and in the furniture of our houses, industrious in our occupations, just in all our dealings, and ever ready to honor all men. Let us teach our children the rudiments of the English language, in order to enable them to acquire a knowledge of useful trades, and, above all things, let us instruct them in the principles of the gospel of Jesus Christ, whereby they may become raised unto salvation. It has always been a mystery, Why the impartial Father of the human race should have permitted the transportation of so many millions of our fellow creatures to this country, to endure all the miseries of slavery. Perhaps his design was, that a knowledge of the gospel might be acquired by some of their descendants, in order that they might become qualified to be the messengers of it, to the land of their fathers. Let this thought animate us, when we are teaching our children to love and adore the name of our Redeemer. Who knows but that a Joseph may rise up among them, who shall be the instrument of feeding the African nations with the bread of life, and of saving them, not from earthly bondage, but from the more galling yoke of sin and Satan.

Fourthly, Let us be grateful to our benefactors, who, by enlightening the minds of the rulers of the earth, by means of their publications and remonstrances against the trade in our countrymen, have produced the great event we are this day celebrating. Abolition societies and individuals have equal claims to our gratitude. It would be difficult to mention the names of any of our benefactors, without offending many whom we do not know. Some of them are gone to heaven, to receive the reward of their labours of love towards us; and the kindness and benevolence of the survivors, we hope, are recorded in the book of life, to be mentioned with honour when our Lord shall come to reward his faithful servants before an assembled world.

Fifthly, and lastly, Let the first of January, the day of the abolition of the slave trade in our country, be set apart in every year, as a day of publick thanksgiving for that mercy. Let the history of the sufferings of our brethren, and of their deliverance, descend by this means to our children, to the remotest generations; and when they shall ask, in time to come, saying, What mean the lessons, the psalms, the prayers and the praises in the worship of this day? let us answer them, by saying, the Lord, on the day of which this is the anniversary, abolished the trade which dragged your fathers from their native country, and sold them as bondmen in the United States of America.

Oh thou God of all the nations upon the earth! we thank thee, that thou art no respecter of persons, and that thou halt made of one blood all nations of men. We thank thee, that thou hast appeared, in the fullness of time, in behalf of the nation from which most of the worshipping people, now before thee, are descended. We thank thee, that the sun of righteousness has at last shed his morning beams upon them. Rend thy heavens, O Lord, and come down upon the earth; and grant that the mountains, which now obstruct the perfect day of thy goodness and mercy towards them, may flow down at thy presence. Send thy gospel, we beseech thee, among them. May the nations, which now sit in darkness, behold and rejoice in its light. May Ethiopia soon stretch out her hands unto thee, and lay hold of the gracious promise of thy everlasting covenant. Destroy, we beseech thee, all the false religions which now prevail among them; and grant, that they may soon cast their idols, to the moles and the bats of the wilderness.

O, hasten that glorious time, when the knowledge of the gospel of Jesus Christ, shall cover the earth, as the waters cover the sea; when the wolf shall dwell with the lamb, and the leopard shall lie down with the kid and the calf and the young lion and the fatling together, and a little child shall lead them; and, when, instead of the thorn, shall come up the fir tree, and, instead of the brier, shall come up the myrtle tree: and it shall be to the Lord for a name and for an everlasting sign that shall not be cut off. We pray, O God, for all our friends and benefactors, in Great Britain, as well as in the United States: reward them, we beseech thee, with blessings upon earth, and prepare them to enjoy the fruits of their kindness to us, in thy everlasting kingdom in heaven: and dispose us, who are assembled in thy presence, to be always thankful for thy mercies, and to act as becomes a people who owe so much to thy goodness. We implore thy blessing, O God, upon the President, and all who are in authority in the United States. Direct them by thy wisdom, in all their deliberations, and O save thy people from the calamities of war. Give peace in our day, we beseech thee, O thou God of peace! and grant, that this highly favored country may continue to afford a safe and peaceful retreat from the calamities of war and slavery, for ages yet to come. We implore all these blessings and mercies, only in the name of thy beloved Son, Jesus Christ, our Lord. And now, O Lord, we desire, with angels and arch-angels, and all the company of heaven, evermore to praise thee, saying, Holy, holy, holy, Lord God Almighty: the whole earth is full of thy glory. Amen.

Living with Change

GARDNER C. TAYLOR

I n this world of change and turmoil, constancy can only be found
in God. As he did in his sermon "A Question Out of the Darkness,"
Gardner C. Taylor gives comfort to those facing the inequities and
ephemeral nature of the world today. "Change is the law of our lives,"
he says, but there is a constant in our lives, a "North Star" by which
to steer.

Living with Change

The voice said, Cry. And he said, What shall 1 cry? All flesh is grass, and all the goodliness thereof is as the /lower of the field: The grass withereth, the flower fadeth: because the spirit of the LORD bloweth upon it: surely the people are grass. The grass withereth, the flower fadeth: but the word of our God shall stand forever.

ISAIAH 40:6-8

There seems to be instinctive in us a desire for permanence, constancy, stability. Something in us seems to resist all change. This characteristic is baffling, since it does not grow out of our experience. The environmental psychologists would have to blink and stammer at this one. They say to us that we are the products totally of our experiences. Well, we have ever known anything in this world that lasted. Each moment and minute of time has been a stern summons to keep moving. Time marches on, or is it down, or up? We have ever been on the march, living with change every day of our mortal journey.

Still, we long desperately for permanence and stability. Is it that we are really native to some other clime, originally citizens of some dispensation where shift and change are strange and alien? "Where all o'er those wide extended plains shines one eternal day." Do we come here by way of long human memory from some place where life and circumstance are unthreatened? Where "no chilling winds, no poisonous breath can reach that healthful shore, sickness and sorrow and pain and death are felt and feared no more." Was Wordsworth on truth's target when he said, "Trailing clouds of glory do we come from God who is our home?"

Whatever the case, we have to live with change. There are various versions of an instructive little story. One account of this widely told tale's origin has it that Warren Hastings related it to some friends at the time of his trial in England. A monarch, so the tale runs, who suffered many hours of discouragement urged his courtiers to devise a motto short enough to be engraved on a ring, which should be suitable alike in prosperity and adversity. After many suggestions had been rejected, his daughter offered an emerald bearing the inscription in Arabic: "This, too, shall pass away." And so, whatever it is, it shall. We must learn to live with change.

Isaiah spoke in his lovely musical fortieth chapter of the transitoriness of all that is on earth as over against the unchangeableness of God. Israel was enduring a bitter slavery. Her oppressors seemed invulnerable and unconquerable. Babylon had built a mighty empire. Her star in its ascendancy seemed so bright that it could never decline in brilliance and power. The downcast and dispirited exiles by Babylon's streams could not help feeling overawed and forever helpless in the face of the great military juggernaut and the economic colossus which held them as slaves in the iron grip of its powerful hand.

As they looked around at the splendor of the architecture and masonry of Babylon, these slaves must have felt very small and insignificant. These poor Israelite captives had seen the wondrous hanging gardens of Babylon, called one of the wonders of the ancient world. Tradition says that these hanging gardens were composed of trees and flowers planted upon terraces, one upon the other, to a height of one hundred fifty feet and watered by means of a device similar to an invention of Archimedes. The humble, ill-clad slaves looking at this dazzling sight must have felt a terrible despair and an aching longing for home. Their melancholy cry cuts at the heart as they lamented. "By the waters of Babylon, there we sat down, yea, we wept, when we remembered Zion." The society among which they were aliens and slaves was so highly developed and so intricately accomplished in literature and commerce and business. Modern excavations reveal an amazing body of literature carefully catalogued like a modern library. Babylon's tax structure was elaborate and sophisticated, and her deeds and mortgages and bills of sale attest to a highly developed culture. What could some slaves mean midst all these achievements when they had only some exotic ways of worship and an invisible God upon whom to call midst the galling yoke and heavy oppression of their captivity?

The unknown prophet of the exile whom we call Isaiah took one look at all of this heathen splendor and pagan power and saw the fatal void at the heart of it all. Isaiah saw a deep and awful night, unillumined by the true and living God, at the very center of the bright achievements of Babylon culture. The prophet saw the mighty architecture of Babylonian power, unsupported by the Rock of Ages but erected upon shifting sand and treacherous soil. His voice rises like a trumpet of doom and hope midst the scattered dreams and sagging morale of God's own people. "All flesh is grass, and all the goodliness thereof is as the flower of the field."

"Never mind," he must have mused, "how green and lush the grass may seem. Never mind how bright and picturesque the blossoming flowers may appear." Then he went on, "The grass withereth, the flower fadeth." Let every person who stands in failure or success take note of this word. In the hour of failure we are likely to feel that all is lost, that we have come upon some endless desert, and for us there is no deliverance. People's hearts in such hours fail them with fear. It takes a mighty courage to keep on marching when the journey seems endless and the pilgrimage seems hopeless. We can bear almost anything—personal misfortune, sickness, injustice, poverty, whatever—as long as we have some assurance as to when and how it will end. The sword passes to the heart when trudging in a weary and rough way we see no sign of relief, no end, not even a turning. It is then that we are likely to feel a deep, numbing despair.

A gasp of admiration crosses the spirit when we think of people who have been able to look through their fears and peer through their heartbreak to the faith that nothing in this world remains the same. "I'm so glad trouble don't last always," some people desperately circumstanced once said, and found bright claws for their deep night. On the other hand, the man who stands in the heady moment of success needs to hear the prophet's words.

When things go well with us, we tend to believe that the sun will always shine. Of course, we ought not to be constantly looking for a blow to fall, for sober tidings which snatch the breath away and leave us stunned and gasping. At the same time, in the day of calm, we ought while enjoying the quiet beauty, set ourselves for the time of storm and fury. We want our high and happy moments to go on forever. We do not want our privileged status in society changed. We want always to be praised and lauded and honored. We do not want to see our neighborhoods change. We want our church to remain the same. This is a vain longing.

Change is the law of our lives, and we cannot maintain anything as we would have it. We are sailing on a restless sea. The voyage does not remain the same. We are going forward, or we are driven back. White-capped waves dash to and fro. There is endless, restless change on this bounding tempestuous sea. There are no permanent markers. The moon pulls at the sea, and the winds whip the waters. How shall we steer? By what shall we mark our way?

To change the prophet's figure but not his truth, look up. Midst all this change there is a star. It is the North Star. For those who live in the northern hemisphere, the Pole Star is the one heavenly light which does not change position. The old sailors sailed by it. Wind and sun and moon and constellations shifted, but the North Star stayed in place. Even now the navigator must test his compass by the reliable constancy of the North Star.

Quickly now, do you see the answer to the whole thing? How odd of us not to notice that there is an answer, sure and certain, to our longing for abidingness. It really does not need any comment from me. "The grass withereth, the flower fadeth; but the word of our God shall stand for ever." There, there is your North Star. Steer carefully and steadily by it.

Wisdom in Work

CAROL ANN NORTH

I n "Wisdom in Work," Carol Ann North shows us that lessons can be drawn from everyday life; lessons that are echoed in religious scripture. This sermon was first preached to seminary students at the Princeton Theological Seminary in Princeton, New Jersey. It serves as an inspiration and life lesson not only for those working to attain a life within the ministry, but to those who labor each day. No matter how humble the work, North points out, there is wisdom to be gained from it.

Wisdom in Work

Having worked in a social service organization in Chicago as an employment counselor, I discovered that hundreds of people work at jobs that pay them well but do not fulfill them. In fact, some people hated the work that they did but felt bound and trapped by their work because of financial rewards. We as women and men often work our way to the grave.

I want to challenge us as seminary students to think about work in the context of this Ecclesiastes text in which the writer, known as Qohelet, offers his philosophical insight about work. Not only does Qohelet explore human toil; he also examines labor's rewards and life's endings.

Qohelet declares in Ecclesiastes 2:17, "So I hated life, because what is done under the sun was grievous to me; for all is vanity and striving after wind." Is this our sentiment about the work that we do? Perhaps for so many of God's children such works do resonate with their sense of work's daily grind in a demanding capitalistic society. Do we grumble while getting out of bed, day in and day out, to go to jobs that we disdain? Even when we work in our respective churches, doing all types of ministries, do we sometimes wonder if we are just striving after the wind? In what ways do we share Qohelet's complaint about the void that we find in life's labor—yes, even in the church? Do we ponder with him the elusive abundant life and wonder if all that we're doing is really all for nothing?

Was Qohelet any different from us? Wasn't he just someone who worked and looked for meaning in work and for some reward? So what was it that brought him to the point where he said, "I hated all my toil in which I had toiled under the sun, seeing that I must leave it to the man who will come after me; and who knows whether he will be a wise man or a fool? Yet he will be master of all for which I toiled and used my wisdom under the sun." Qohelet is upset. After he has sweated and toiled, his wealth could end up going to another undeserving soul to enjoy. In fact, he says, his fortune could end up in the hands of a fool. No wonder he doesn't have anything good to say about work and labor's rewards.

I believe that Qohelet is very much like us. He really wants to know what the future holds. On his journey, he wants to look down the road, see every stop that lies ahead, and see what the end will be. He wants to know what will become of his power, his prestige, and his money. He, like us, wants to know what God is doing with our future. What's more, he wants to know whether he can assign his own reward to this life, with all of its trappings, trials, and tales.

In seminary, we study theology, the Bible, ethics, congregational ministry, preaching pastoral care, and more. We gain greater insight and wisdom about the meaning of the "work" that we must do in full-time ministry in which we wish to specialize—or maybe our studies have revealed to us that we do not want to continue in ministry. I submit to you that whatever we take or leave from our studies in seminary, we will find that we need much wisdom in the work that lies ahead.

In ministry, we will find women and men who want to discuss with us their frustrations about their work. They will want us to give them words of wisdom on being good stewards of their money. They will tell us how much they want to enjoy the labor of their head, hands, and heart and their concerns about doing a will to be prepared when it's all over.

Before we can provide meaningful counsel to others, we must wrestle with out own ideas regarding life's work, life's reward, and life's end. We must search our hearts to know whether we see work as futile, money as fleeting, and death as the end. Qohelet stirs our conscience and compels us to decide if we see our own lives as fruitful, faithful, and fearless. His words warn us to be careful because we could end up hating our work and feeling that it is ultimately worthless.

Let's go down to the Gulf Coast of Mississippi. There we find one who can us dome wisdom about work. Her name is Oseola McCarty. Her career title was not doctor, not lawyer, not preacher; she was a washerwoman. Oseola washed clothes by hand—abandoning the washer and drying in the '60s because she did not believe that this machinery washed clothes clean enough.

For seventy-five years, day after day, Oseola washed and ironed other people's clothes. She started out being paid fifty cents a day, but she still did her best. Perhaps she followed Martin Luther King's advice: "If it falls your lot in life to be a . . . [washerwoman, wash clothes] like Michelangelo painted the Sistine Chapel." Oseola, following King's directive, offers Qohelet and us another voice about wisdom in work.

Oseola taught us wisdom in work because she transcended the claims in this Ecclesiastes text. She transformed the common chore of washing other people's clothes. Then she transferred her life savings to an educational institution, where generations could become empowered through knowledge. Oseola understood Ecclesiastes 2:25: "For to the man [or woman] who please him God gives wisdom and knowledge and joy; but to the sinner he gives the work of gathering and heaping, only to give to one who pleases God."

I believe that God loaned Oseola to us for such a season in the world as this. Oseola speaks to Qohelet and us out of one of the most mundane jobs that we know about, washing clothes. This gentle giant—who never drove a car and who walked everywhere—is a stellar example to the world's workers of what our lives yield if we are loyal to our labor and use wisdom with our rewards.

Oseola washed clothes in Mississippi under the sizzling sun, saved nearly a quarter of a million dollars, and donated it to the University of Southern Mississippi. She lived her life in a way that made her happy to get up in the morning and go to work. She didn't wake up grumbling and saying like Ecclesiastes 2:23, "[Our] days are full of pain, and...[our] work is a vexation; even in the night... [our] mind does not rest." Even though she has only a sixth-grade education—having dropped out of school to care for her loved ones—she learned something that our academic institutions might never teach us. She learned how to work wisely, live simply, and give generously. Oseola offered her work and her life to a culture of corrupt capitalists.

Oseola did not stand before classrooms of students, nor did she preach before the president. She just washed clothes. She washed clothes that scratched her fingers and bruised her hands. Before there were whiteners and brighteners, she washed clothes. Sometimes on her knees using a scrub board, she washed clothes. And she ironed collars and cuffs and saved her dimes and dollars.

And unlike many of us, Oseola did not work to buy, travel, taste, splurge, and partake. She worked to bless, and she did bless this generation. But she also blessed those to come. As they study to earn their degrees, they profit from Oseola learned in her labor and her leisure.

As we minister to women and men who are frustrated and unfulfilled in their work, we can point them to the life Oseola. We can help them to discover just how meaningful any task can be when we seek the wisdom of God in what we do. We can help ourselves and others know that our work and the money we earn should not be used just to satisfy our every creature comfort.

Can you imagine a world in which most live and work as Oseola did? Oseola's life is exemplary of the true meaning of learning to live as Jesus taught to live—preferring others and we do ourselves. Wherever the history of Mississippi is told and the story of this washwoman is repeated, Oseola will be an example of one who knew how to work for a greater good and better end. Oseola rewarded her human family by being faithful to the work that God gave her hands, her heart, and her head to do. She informed our work ethos with her unprecedented example of wisdom about work.

Oseola did not read the economist forecast, the sociologist's date, or the theologian's commentaries on how to work, save, and give. Perhaps she did read part of Ecclesiastes and differed with it. She showed us that you can love the work that you do, do it with tremendous pride, and share your earnings so that they can bless others.

The response to her wisdom about work rests in all the newspaper editorials following her death. The media could hardly capture the outpouring of respect, admiration, and exhilaration for the legacy of Oseola McCarty. Oseola believed that mortals get something far greater for their toil and strain than Qohelet ever imagined. Oseola refused to accept that her work was mundane and ignored.

God used the life of Oseola McCarty to give us new insight into this Ecclesiastes text. Through her splendid example we can find greater love for our labor, thanksgiving in our toil, wisdom in our work. By doing this, we can also enrich the lives of others through the work God gives our hands, our head, and our heart to do. This is why the old folk song,

> If I can help somebody, as I travel along,
> If I can cheer somebody with a word or a son,
> Then my living will not be in vain.
> . . . then my living will not be in vain.
> Then my living will not be in vain.

Prayer Power:
Jesus on the Mainline

WYATT TEE WALKER

In "Prayer Power," Wyatt Tee Walker once again turns a scholarly eye to a traditional hymn, "Jesus On the Mainline." In his careful analysis, Walker shows the power and affirmation of faith that resides in "earnest prayer" in our lives.

Prayer Power:
Jesus on the Mainline

Jesus on the mainline,
Tell Him what you want.
Jesus on the mainline,
Tell Him what you want.
Jesus on the mainline,
Tell Him what you want.
Jesus on the mainline now!

If you want more power,
Tell Him what you want.
If you want more power,
Tell Him what you want.
If you want more power,
Tell Him what you want.
Jesus on the mainline now!

If you want the Holy Ghost,
Tell Him what you want.
If you want the Holy Ghost,
Tell Him what you want.

If you want the Holy Ghost,
Tell Him what you want.
Jesus on the mainline now!

Call Him up, call Him UP,
Tell Him what you want.
Call Him up, call Him up,
Tell Him what you want.
Call Him up, call Him up,
Tell Him what you want.
Jesus on the mainline now!

INTRODUCTION

This Prayer and Praise Hymn enjoys wide recognition in the family
of Afro-American Christians. As in the instance of You Can't Make
Me Doubt Him, this hymn can be "raised" anywhere among Black
Christians and it will be sung with great fervor and meaning. The
word imagery suggests strongly that it is of late vintage for this class
of music. The reader will recall from the Introduction to this volume
that the time-frame of the development of this music is from the end
of the last century to the beginning of World War I. The "mainline"
reference along with "call Him up" are obvious allusions to telephone
technology. If as set forth, the bulk of this musical literature is rural
in origin, then familiarity with party-line telephone would of necessity have come in the latter part of the period suggested.

It is precisely this "mainline" reference which sets this hymn
apart from most of the others in this genre. Not very many of this
grouping reflect the unique imagery often present in its forerunner,
the Spiritual. The antebellum slaves drew from their surroundings—
the word pictures to illustrate some specific aspect of their faith.
"Keep inchin' along like a po' inch worm" is an example that comes
immediately to mind. In a later era, these descendants of slaves drew

from their surroundings and fastened upon the telephone as a means of conveying to the Lord their hopes and aspirations. Generally speaking, in both the Spirituals and these hymns, the practice was to lean heavily upon the imagery gleaned from the Scriptures. Occasionally, they created images from their contemporary surroundings as in the respective' instances cited above.

The central idea of this faith-hymn is that Jesus is available and figuratively speaking, He is only a phone call away.

BIBLICAL BASIS

Once again this hymn demonstrates the peculiar musical genius of the ordinary people who created this body of music. It has been asserted in another place in this work that the bench-mark of that genius is the manner in which the collective folk-mind distilled profound theological ideas into convenient and sometimes quaint vehicles of transmission for the faith-community. It must be remembered that there was no broad ground of literacy for these early saints to stand upon. Barely half of the Black population in the entire South could read and write and in the rural where these hymns were born, the statistics for literacy were markedly lower. It can be deduced that much of their Biblical knowledge was hearsay at best. The genius of the music is whatever they read or heard, they made splendid use of both.

We can surmise that the Biblical basis of this hymn is centered in the late admonition of Jesus to his disciples:

> Verily, verily I say unto you,
> Whatsoever ye shall ask the Father
> in my name, he will give it to you.

At the heart of this hymn is the confidence in prayer. There is also an additional consideration that this hymn betrays an inherent characteristic of the religious practice of Christians of African ancestry, the centrality of Jesus. Indeed, the music, past and present; the prayers, the preaching, the theological stance—all are dominated by the person of the Lord Jesus Christ. In the slave era, this pronounced emphasis gave rise to the description of the practice of religion among the New World Africans as the "Jesus-faith."

The theme of this hymn is of course, prayer. Our forbearers of this historical period accepted with little question the power of prayer for the individual and/or the community of faith. Their confidence in prayer was grounded in the New Testament record of the life and practice of Jesus and in the Gospels and the tradition of the Early Church. They deciphered the importance of prayer from what they read in the Bible and what they heard the Bible say about prayer. It was the prayer life of our Lord which impressed the disciples of Jesus most. "Lord, teach us to pray" is in sharp contrast to the absence of the disciples request to be taught to preach or to heal. That which is of most importance is the discernment of the originators of this hymn to express their absolute confidence in the power and efficacy of prayer.

The traditional prayers of the Afro-American religious experience frequently include the phrase, "Lord teach us to pray and what to pray for . . . " Though it is a cliche of prayer, it has sound instruction for all believers. Too many professing Christians misuse the discipline of prayer. The error of much of our praying is that we wish to bend God's will to our will, instead of blending our will to His will. The Model Prayer which Jesus provided in response to His disciples' request provides an adequate and instructive framework for Christian prayer. It is in the spirit of the so called Lord's Prayer that this hymn was framed. The folk mind determined that whatever was needed required only the proper petition and supplication to Jesus. He's on the "mainline" and "tell Him what you want" exudes the unwavering confidence of the petitioners.

The theological significance of this hymn resides in the overall meaning of the prayer discipline to believing Christians. Prayer is communion with the Eternal God. It is the means by which the individual lifts the most heartfelt desires of the soul. It is not always spoken: sometimes it is sung in the words of an appropriate hymn and frequently it is non-verbal. It can be so deep and earnest that only the heart can speak (figuratively) to the Lord.

Prayer moves on the wings of faith. If the petitioner does not believe his/her prayers will be answered, they will not be answered. All earnest prayers to God are answered. The true believer understands the nature Cod's sovereignty. We cannot be so presumptuous to think that God can only answer "Yes!" to our prayers; that would be an abdication of His goodness. God has the right and, the prerogative to say to any and all of His children, "Yes," "No" or "Wait." There are probably more "No" answers because so much of our praying is outside the discipline of genuine Christian prayer.

The instruction of Jesus to "ask in my name" is more than formula. It is the clear mandate that prayer would not be reduced to ordering from a menu. True prayer must be intelligent and devoid of our hyperactive ego drives. The verbiage of our prayers need increasingly to be more "Make me . . ." than "Give me . . . ."

A glaring absence in our prayer conduct is "Thank you Lord." The trial and tribulation syndrome crowds out the continuing need to thank God as did the Shunamite woman. Her heart was breaking with grief and sorrow when Elisha's body servant inquired about her welfare and that of her husband and son. She replied, "It is well" meaning that each circumstance in my life is not as I desire but I thank God that things are as well as they are. That is an appropriate prayer posture.

LYRIC AND FORM ANALYSIS

The poetic form of this hymn is a slight variant to what we have considered in this study. It is different enough not to fit into the mold of any of the hymns reviewed to date.

a Jesus on the mainline,
b Tell Him what you want.
a Jesus on the mainline,
b Tell Him what you want.
a Jesus on the mainline,
b Tell Him what you want.
c Jesus on the mainline now!

In strict poetic analysis, the c line might not be considered a different line since the only difference is the word, "now." However, in order to be consistent with the previous analyses, I have opted to designate it as a new line in order to differentiate both the literary form and allow for the adjustment in the melodic line. Thus, this variant form becomes a b a b a b c and is unlike any previously considered.

The variant noted is the chief distinguishing characteristic. All others seem to obtain. The melody is straightforward, uncomplicated and repetition abounds. Easy access to performance and participation are enhanced by the traditional profile of this genre of music.

The stanzas replicate the form of the refrain. The only change is in the words without any violence to the basic form of the melodic structure or poetic design. The stanzas maintain the variant a b a b a b c exactly. As in most of this music, the central thrust of the message is contained in the refrain and the slight word changes in the stanzas are ornamentation. This is not to suggest that the message of the stanzas is unimportant. They merely amplify the central message enunciated in the refrain. It is of some note to consider the items inserted to create the stanzas. "More power," of course, refers to the capacity to live as a Christian and "the Holy Ghost" is the traditional and religio-cultural statement about the means by which triumphant living is achieved.

CONTEMPORARY SIGNIFICANCE

The quaint character of this hymn might easily obscure the serious-ness of its profundity. Modern devotees of the religion of Jesus are often tempted into some sort of fatalism; a resignation to whatever comes, without sincere faith in the power of effective prayer. The other side of the coin is that quarter of the family of faith who unwittingly wish to make a glorified bellboy out of the Lord. The long litany of requests for what we want without sufficient discernment about what we need are often outside the pale of what Christian prayer should be. The lack of positive response to these kinds of petitions have induced the fatalism mentioned above. We have too little faith in the prayers we pray to be answered by the Lord whom we profess to serve.

This Prayer and Praise Hymn, if carefully scrutinized contains the trust element so essential to earnest prayer. The traditional stance of the Afro-American religious: experience is an unequivocal belief that God answers prayer. This hymn, in spite of its quaintness, lifts up that very same abiding truth. To sing this hymn with trust and confide in its message is an affirmation of what one believe; the power of prayer in our lives.

Calling for the Order of the Day
NUMBERS 13:25-33

KATIE G. CANNON

K atie Geneva Cannon is the first African American woman to be ordained in the United Presbyterian Church in the U.S.A., to earn a Ph.D. from Union Theological Seminary in New York. Cannon presently teaches religion at Temple University in Philadelphia, and is the author of several books on Christian ethics. In her "Calling For the Order of the Day," Cannon is eloquently urging us all to put aside victimhood, put aside our day-to-day concerns, and our notions of a past that is better than the present. Only then, she proclaims jubilantly, can we love God and discover fulfillment, freedom, and happiness.

Calling for the Order of the Day
NUMBERS 13:25-33

I ndeed, there are so many directions in which we might focus our attention in the countdown to the new millennium, but in "calling for the order of the day" we prioritize our Christian mission. "Calling for the order of the day" means that we preempt everything else that is going on around us and return to the designated item on the covenantal docket. "Calling for the order of the day" means that with dispatch all discussion must cease, all filibustering must stop, all superfluous appendages must be dispensed with, because we have no time to lose. "Calling for the order of the day" is the divine command for us to return to the pressing, indispensable, urgent prerequisite that is our God-given imperative—to do justice, to love mercy, and to walk humbly with our God. So I say to each and everyone, as we enter the twenty-first century, it is time for us to call for the order of the day.

In the book of Numbers, the thirteenth chapter, verses 25-33, we find our scriptural sermon focus. Numbers is a sacred historical text. It deals with beginnings, origins, the birth of the people of God. And as we cross the threshold into the year 2000, it is of utmost importance for us to zero in on this particular sermonic text.

In Numbers we find the people of God grumbling and complaining about bread from heaven, fussing and fuming in their trek to the land of promise. And according to the textural background in Numbers 13, we find that the freed people of God have already crossed the desert. They are out of the wildness. They now stand at the foot of the mountain in Paran, at Kadesh, and on the other side of the mountain is Canaan, the land that God promises to give to them.

So God tells Moses to send out twelve spies so that they can assess the situation. Thus Moses calls for the order of the day by selecting a representative from each of the tribes and gives them a checklist as to what data they need to gather so that the people could successfully enter the Promised Land. Moses told the scouts to examine the lifestyle of the people; to take note of the geographical features of the land; and to pay attention to the people's strengths and weaknesses, whether the inhabitants were large in number or just a few, whether the towns were unwalled or well fortified. All in all, Moses said for the twelve tribal representatives to stay alert to everything around them. Being that this was the time of year for the ripening of grapes, Moses requested that the spies also bring back some fruit.

In a modern-day amplified translation of Numbers 13:25-33, this is what it says:

> After forty days, the twelve spies returned from searching out of the land. They came to Moses, Aaron and to all the people in the congregation. They brought back word concerning how the land flowed with mild and honey; how the people who dwell in this new land are strong and the cities are well fortified. To convince the people of the fertility of Canaan, the spies brought some pomegranates and figs for the assembly. A single cluster of grapes was so big and heavy that two spies had to carry the grapes on a pole between them. And, it was at this point that the assembled congregation began to lift up their voices, weeping aloud and crying out.

But Caleb quieted the people before Moses. Caleb called for the order of the day. Caleb said to the congregation, "Let us go up at once and occupy the land, this land that is exceedingly good because God is on our side and we are well able to overcome all that is there."

Then ten of the spies who had gone with Caleb argued, "We are not able to go up against the people of Canaan, for they are stronger than we are." In our modern-day parlance, they said, "The Canaanites will smash us to smithereens." In the negative report by the majority of scouts, the spies told the congregation that the people in Canaan were cannibals, devouring their inhabitants. "The Canaanites are huge in stature, so much so that they are giants and we, ourselves, seem like grasshoppers."

It was at this point that the people of God cried louder. The congregation wept throughout the night. While moaning and murmuring against Moses and Aaron, members of the congregation asked, "Why did God not let us die in slavery? Why could we not have died in the wilderness? Why did Yahweh bring us to this foreign land to be killed by giants? Would it not be better for us if we go back to Egypt?" And it was at this point that the people said, one to another, "Let us choose a captain, and go back to Egypt." Then Moses and Aaron fell on their faces before all the assembly of the congregation of Israel.[1]

Sisters and brothers, as we worship here near the beginning of a new century, just like the people in our Bible lesson, far too many of us want to follow the crowd and live in the past whenever we hear unfavorable reports concerning our situation, simply because we lack courage when it comes to calling for the order of the day. As we contemplate the challenges presented by the new millennium, so many

---

1. Numbers 14:1-4

of us find ourselves busily looking back into the good old bygone days, yearning for yesteryears when the living seemed easy and the cotton was high, rather than joyously anticipating God's unfolding promises.

As church folks gathered together in worship, we begin anew, with endless possibilities before us. Yet, far too many of us are still shackled by grasshopper mentalities. We cling to the negative majority report that says over and over again that we are too little in the world of scientific investigations; we are too weak when it comes to grasping medical knowledge; we are insufficient in relations to the global economy; we are inadequate, merely roadkill, on the cyberspace superhighway of the Worldwide Web; we are incompetent whenever it comes to the business that God is calling for each of us to do. And when we start believing that we are really grasshoppers and that the world around us is inhabited by giants, then we end up internalizing a degenerating sense of nobody-ness. In turn, we rape our own psyche, convincing ourselves that the return to slavery is a return to "the way we were," to the so-called good old days, when the winters were warmer, the grass was greener, the skies were bluer, and the smiles were brighter.

However, Randall Kenan in his new book, Walking on Water: Black American Lives at the Turn of the Twenty-first Century, sums up the why-crises of this type of romanticized, death-dealing miseducation:

It is much too easy: to make poverty holy; to make ugliness beautiful; to make violence valiant; to make weakness charming; to make stupidity wise; to make arrogance comic; to make disease health; to make squalor exotic; to make meanness noble; to make cruelty ingenious; to make stink perfume; to make laziness expression; to make anger pride; to make debauchery art; to make nothing something; to make blindness sight; to make evil good.

Therefore, dearly beloved, since we see that the deadly effects of continually embracing a grasshopper mentality will be that we forfeit our right to the unfolding of God's future promises, let us embrace the virtues of beauty, goodness, and truth related to the calling for the order of the day. This is necessary in order for us to possess the courage to live meaningful lives in the name of our God and our Creator, now, henceforth, and forever.

The first element we must embrace related to calling for the order of the day is beauty. Most of us have heard the age-old saying, "Beauty is in the eye of the beholder." And the truth of this statement requires each of us to lift up, to shine the spotlight on, and to accentuate the positive people, places, and things in our lives today. Too often we get hung up focusing on crime and corruption, abuse and misuse, powers and principalities, and we devote very little time, if any, to being grateful for the blessed opportunities to be a better Christian today than we were yesterday. Behold the beauty of each new opportunity.

We must take time away, far from the madding crowd, and seriously examine our ultimate concern, our master motives, the supreme determiner of who we are and who we want to become. Those of us who have made a decision to be disciples of Jesus Christ need to search into the bottom chambers of our hearts, into those places in the core of our being where we tend to hide our worries and anxieties, our secrets and our shame, our fears and our angst, and evaluate the truth of God in our lives. Instead of grumbling and complaining about the staleness of today's bread, let us cultivate an attitude of gratitude regarding the manna from heaven that God gives to us morning by morning. Behold the beauty of each moment.

Just like Moses in our Scripture lesson, we too must send out representatives, antennae, all kinds of feelers, as we assess the future situations that await us. The spies had to find out exactly the strengths and weaknesses of the people who inhabited the land. And after they collected their data, Moses told them to return and report their fact-finding to the assembled congregation. Likewise, each of us must do soul-searching personal inventories. What are our strengths? What are our weaknesses? Exactly what are the gifts and graces that God has already bestowed upon us in preparation for Christian living in the twenty-first century? To embrace beauty means that we diligently examine our personal situation, calling for the order in each new day.

The second element we must embrace related to calling for the order of the day is goodness. Goodness is quality and quantity. When we embrace goodness, we take hold of our integrity in the context of community. Goodness means that we do not spread ourselves too thin, boxing at the wind. Goodness enables us to practice self-control so that we limit the number of irons in life's fire. Yes, Church, goodness is the state of mind that makes us aware of our finiteness, our own right-sizeness.

When we embrace beauty, we touch base with our God-given birthright, that daily aspect of our being that is always preparing the way for the future. And this second element of goodness requires us to accept the findings of our personal inventory. In other words, we must admit that there have been times in the past when we did not partake of the grapes, pomegranates, and figs that our foreparents risked their lives to bring to us. Like the members of the assembled congregation in our Scripture lesson who heard the minority report as well as the majority report, we must admit that there have been times when we too have pushed God out of our lives as we wailed, moaned, murmured, and cried all through the night.

Others of us must accept the various ways that we have waddled in denial, so much so that slavery looked like freedom. And a few of us must accept the honest revelation that we have been the ringleaders in our families, among our friends, and in the church community who selected captains—pastors, elders, deacons, and trustees—to take us back to wander in the wilderness of nobody-ness. Yes, goodness is the inward resolution that gives us confidence to accept the findings in our rigorous self-inventory in calling for the order of the day.

The other element we must embrace related to calling for the order of the day is truth. We must humble ourselves before God in prayer in order to discern what reports are God-given and what reports are people-given. The only way that any of us can get to the Promised Land is that we must let go of our slave mentality and learn to depend on the true and living God. If we want things to be well with our souls, if we want to be free, if we want to be whole, then day by day we must let go and let God show us the way.

Caleb insists on calling for the order of the day in his minority report. To the extent that we surrender our lives to God's care, to the extent that we get out of our own way, to that very extent is when God's truth takes root, strengthening us where we are weak, building us up where we are torn down. In such moments of truth we are able by God's grace to renounce the sins of the past and experience God's forgiveness of our bygone days. In such moments of truth, we establish genuine prayerful communication with almighty God. The women and men in our Biblical text who refused to heed the call for the order of the day proved to be disobedient, and in turn they never saw the land that was a promised to them through their ancestors. But Caleb—he and his descendents would eventually enter the Promised Land.

In such moments of truth, we, like Caleb, rid ourselves of whatever may distract our minds in the present and encumber our living in the future. Yes, at the core of our God-fearing lives we must hold on to divine truth, an irresistible, dogged determination to persevere, to get to the land of promise. We must be driven by God's truth, not by truths created by human minds that cannot dream dreams that are big enough for the destinies that God has in store for us.

Now, I invite each of you to join the cloud of twenty-first century witnesses in calling for the order of the day. Calling for the order of the day requires that you embrace your inner beauty and love yourself. Calling for the order of the day requires that you take hold of goodness, which boils down to doing an honest inventory that will allow us to be in harmony with God, our neighbor, and our best selves. And in calling for the order of the day, let us never forget the final element of divine truth, which can be summer up in the greatest commandment—to love the Lord God with all our heart, mind, soul, and strength. I wholeheartedly believe that when we embrace beauty, goodness, and truth, our lives will be fulfilled, our living will not be in vain, our unique potential will be actualized, morning by morning and ay by day. Madam Moderator, Mister Moderator, I call for the order of the day!

The Eagle Stirreth Her Nest

C.L. FRANKLIN

Although perhaps most frequently remembered as the father of singer Aretha Franklin, Charles L. Franklin was the inspiration for thousands at his New Bethel Baptist Church in Detroit, Michigan, and with his Franklin's Gospel Caravan, a traveling evangelical group. He himself recorded seventy-six albums of gospel songs and music, and worked not only to inspire, but also to correct injustice. In 1963, he organized a freedom march in Detroit, marching side by side with Martin Luther King Jr.

The power of Franklin's oratory is evident in "The Eagle Stirreth Her Nest," a sermon that in many ways harks back to the emotive preachers of earlier days.

The Eagle Stirreth Her Nest

The eagle here is used to symbolize God's care and God's concern for his people. Many things have been used as symbolic expressions to give us a picture of God or some characteristic of one of his attributes; the ocean, with her turbulent majesty; the mountains, the lions. Many things have been employed as pictures of either God's strength or God's power or God's love or God's mercy. And the psalmist has said that The heavens declare the glory of God and the firmament shows forth his handiworks.

So the eagle here is used as a symbol of God. Now in picturing God as an eagle stirring her nest, I believe history has been one big nest that God has been externally stirring to make man better and to help us achieve world brotherhood. Some of the things that have gone on in your own experiences have merely been God stirring the nest of your circumstances. Now the Civil War, for example, and the struggle in connection with it, was merely the promptings of Providence to lash man to a point of being brotherly to all men. In fact, all of the wars that we have gone through, we have come out with new outlooks and new views and better people. So that throughout history, God has been stirring the various nests of circumstances surrounding us, so that he could discipline us, help us to know ourselves, and help s to love another, and to help us hasten on the realization of the kingdom of God.

The eagle symbolizes God because there is something about an eagle that is a fit symbol of things about God. In the first place,, the eagle is the king of fowls. And if he is a regal or kingly bird, in that majesty he represents the kingship of God or symbolizes the kingship of God. (Listen if you please.) For God is not merely a king, he is the king. Somebody has said that he is the king of kings. For you see, these little kings that we know, they've got to have a king over them. They've got to account to somebody for the deeds done in their bodies. For God is the king. And if the eagle is a kingly bird, in that way he symbolizes the regalness and kingliness of our God.

In the second place, the eagle is strong. Somebody has said that as the eagle goes winging his way through the air he can look down on a young lamb grazing by a mountainside, and can fly down and just with the strength of his claws, pick up this young lamb and fly away to yonder's cleft and devour it—because he's strong. If the eagle is strong, then, in that he is a symbol of God, for our God is strong. Our God is strong. Somebody has called him a fortress. So that when the enemy is pursuing me I can run behind him. Somebody has called him a citadel of protection and redemption. Somebody else has said the he's so strong until they call him a leaning–post that thousands can lean on him, and he'll never get away. (I don't believe you're praying with me.) People have been leaning on him ever since time immemorial. Abraham leaned on him. Isaac and Jacob leaned on him. Moses and the prophets leaned on him. All the Christians leaned on him. People are leaning on him all over the world today. He's never given way. He's strong. That's strong. Isn't it so?

In the second place, he's swift. The eagle is swift. And it is said that he could fly wit such terrific speed that his wings can be heard rowing in the air. He's swift. And if he's swift in that way, he's a symbol of our God. For our God is swift. I said he's swift. Sometimes, sometimes he'll answer you while you're calling him. He's swift. Daniel was thrown in a lions' den. And Daniel rung him on the way to the lions' den. And having rung him, why, God had dispatched the angel from heaven. And by the time that Daniel got to the lions' den, the angel had changed the nature of lions and made them lay down and act like lambs. He's swift, Swift. One night Peter was put in jail and the church went down on its knees to pray for him. And while the church was praying. Peter knocked on the door. God was so swift in answering prayer. So that if the eagle is a swift bird, in that way he represents or symbolizes the fact that God is swift. He's swift. If you get in earnest tonight and tell him about your troubles, he's swift to hear you. All you do is need a little faith, and ask him in grace.

Another things about the eagle is that he has extraordinary sight. Extraordinary sight. Somewhere it is said that he can rise to a lofty height in the air and look in the distance and see a storm hours away. That's extraordinary sight. And sometimes he can stand and gaze right in the sun because he has extraordinary sight. I want to tell you my God has extraordinary sight. He can see every ditch that you have dug for me and guide me around them. God has extraordinary sight. He can look behind that smile on your face and see that frown in your heart. God has extraordinary sight.

Then it is said that an eagle builds a nest unusual. It is said that the eagle selects rough material, basically, for the construction of his nest. And then as the nest graduates toward a close or a finish, the material becomes finer and softer right down at the end. And then he goes about to set up residence in that nest. And when the little eagles are born, she goes out and brings in food to feed them. But when they get to the point where they're old enough to be out on their own, why, the eagle will begin to pull out some that down and let some of those thorns come through so that the nest won't be, you know, so comfortable. So when they get to lounging around and rolling around, the thorns prick 'em here and there. (Pray with me if you please.)

I believe that God has to do that for us sometimes. Things are going so well and we are so satisfied that we just lounge around and forget to pray. You'll walk around all day and enjoy God's life, God's health and God's strength, and go climb into bed without saying, "Thank you, Lord, for another day's journey." We'll do that. God has to pull out a little of the plush around us, a little of the comfort around us, and let a few thorns of trial and tribulation stick through the nest to make us pray sometime. Isn't it so? For most of us forget God when things are going well with us. Most of us forget him.

It is said that there was a ma who had a poultry farm. And that he raised chickens for the market. And one day in one of his broods he discovered a strange looking bird that was very much unlike the other chickens on the yard. [Whooping:]

> And
> the man
>   didn't pay too much attention.
> But he noticed
>   as time went on
> that
> this strange looking bird
>   was unusual.
> He outgrew
>   the other little chickens,
> his habits were stranger
>   and different.
> O Lord.
> But he let him grow on,
> and let him mingle
>   with the other chickens.

O Lord.
And then one day a man
who knew eagles
      when he saw them,
came along
      and saw that little eagle
      walking in the yard.

And
he said to his friend,
"Do you know
      that you have an eagle here?"
The man said, "Well,
      I didn't really know it.
But I knew he was different
      from the other chickens.

And
I knew that his ways
      were different.

And
I knew that his habits
      were different.

And
he didn't act like
      the other chickens.
But I didn't know
      that he was an eagle."
But the man said, "Yes,
      you have an eagle here on your yard.
And what you ought to do
      is build a cage.
After while
when he's a little older

he's going to get tired
of the ground.
Yes he will.
He's going to rise up
on the pinion of his wings.
Yes,
and
as he grows,
why,
you can change the cage,
and
make it a little larger
as he grows older
and grows larger."
The man went out
and built a cage.
And
every day he'd go in
and feed the eagle.
But
he grew
a little older
and a little older.
Yes he did.
His wings
began
to scrape on the sides
of the cage.
And
he had a build
another cage
and open the door of the old cage
and let him into
a larger cage.

Yes he did.
O Lord.
And
  after a while
      he outgrew that one day
      and then he had to build
      another cage.
So one day
      When the eagle had gotten grown,
Lord God,
 and his wings
      were twelve feet
      from tip to tip,
O Lord,
he began to get restless
in the cage.
Yes he did.
He began to walk around
      and he uneasy.
Why,
he, heard
    noises
    in the air.
A flock of eagles flew over
    and he heard
    their voices.
And
though he'd never been around eagles,
there was something about that voice
     that he heard
that moved
     down in him,
and made him
    dissatisfied.

O Lord.
And
the man watched him
    as he walked around
    uneasy.
O Lord.
He said, "Lord,
    my heart goes out to him
I believe I'll go
    and open the door
    and set the eagle free."
O Lord.
He went there
    and opened the door.
Yes.
The eagle walked out,
    yes,
spread his wings,
    then took 'em down.
Yes

The eagle walked around
    a little longer,
and
he flew up a little higher
    and went to the barnyard.
And,
yes,
he set there for a while.
He wiggled up a little higher
and flew in yonder's tree.
Yes.
And then he wiggled up a little higher
and flew to yonder's mountain.

Yes.
Yes!
Yes.
One of these days,
        One of these days
My soul
        is an eagle
in the cage that the Lord
        has made for me.
My soul,
        my soul,
my soul
        is caged in,
        in this old body,
        yes it is,
and one of these days
the man who made the cage
will open the door
and let my soul
        go.
Yes he will.
You ought to
        be able to see me
        that the wings of my soul.
Yes, yes,
yes,
yes!
Yes, one of these days.
One of these old days.
One of these old days.
Did you hear me say it?
I'll fly away
        and be at rest.

Yes.
Yes!
Yes!
Yes!
Yes!
Yes.
One of these old days.

One of these old days.
And
when troubles
          and trials are over,
when toil
          and tears are ended,
when burdens
are through burdening,
Ohh!
Ohh.
Ohh!
Ohh one of these days.
Ohh one of these days.
One of these days.
One of these days.
my soul will take wings,
my soul will take wings,
Ohh!
Ohh, a few more days.
Ohh, a few more days.
A few more days.
O Lord.

A Good Soldier: A Eulogy of Clarence Lavaughn (C. L.) Franklin

JASPER WILLIAMS JR.

E arly on June 10, 1979, burglars broke into the Detroit, Michigan, home of C.L. Franklin. Upon encountering Franklin, the burglars shot and wounded him, sending him into a coma that lasted until his death on July 27, 1984. The father of Aretha Franklin, C.L. Franklin was beloved and admired by many for his stirring, upbeat sermons and his works in the church and in Detroit.

In his eulogy of Franklin, Jasper Williams Jr., senior pastor of Salem Baptist Church of Atlanta, Georgia, combines his own spirit-filled style of preaching with the pastoral energy so typical of Franklin, utilizing "call and response" to stir both listeners and readers.

A Good Soldier: A Eulogy of
Clarence Lavaughn (C. L.) Franklin

From Paul's second letter to Timothy, the second chapter of said book, and the third verse, you'll find the following words: "Thou therefore endure hardness, as a good soldier of Jesus Christ" (KVJ). I want to talk from the subject A Good Soldier, A Good Soldier. [All right. That's all right.]*

At the time that this particular verse was penned, the apostle Paul was awaiting the opportunity to go to Rome and plead his case before Caesar in Rome. Obviously from all indications he had gotten some kind of understanding about the life of the Roman soldier. For many times as he would look out of his barred jail windows he would see soldiers mending, sharpening, and cleaning their weapons. He saw soldiers during drills, soldiers on the march, he saw soldiers on parade. Paul looked and saw soldiers put their armor on and take their armor off. And he detected that the detail of the Roman soldier were very much like the detail of the Christian life and noted

---

* Comments placed in brackets are those of the congregation.

137

how admirably these two entities compared one with another. Therefore when he penned this text to his spiritual son Timothy, he said unto him, "Thou there fore endure hardness, as a good soldier." [Amen. That's right. All right.]

One thing about warfare, as it relates to the Christian life, is that is never an easy fight. [No. That's right.] For whenever one has been loyal and faithful to the gospel, he must be ready to face opposition and ridicule. [Yeah, Yeah.] He must share his suffering with his comrades in arms.

Just stop today and let your mind go back over the saints and prophets of old who have lived and died in this warfare and it will tell us today that it is truly no easy fight.

Stephen was the first deacon of the church. Though full of faith and full of the Holy Ghost, Stephen was stoned to death. [Amen.] Epaphroditus got sick doing the Lord's work. Timothy suffered with stomach trouble. Mathias, who took the place of Judas as one of the Twelve, was killed with a sword in Ethiopia. [Yes sir.] Mark was dragged through the streets of Alexandria. Luke was hanged to death in Greece on a tree. [Well.] John was boiled to death in a kettle of hot burning oil. [Come on.] Peter was crucified on a cross with his head down and his heels up. [Well, my Lord.] Philip was hanged to death, Bartholomew was flogged to death, Barnabas was stoned to death, Paul had his head chopped off at Nero's chopping block. [Yes. Come on preacher.] The Christian fight is no easy fight. [That's right. My Lord.] And I hear him saying to his spiritual son, "Thou therefore endure hardness, as a good soldier."

Notice he said, endure hardness, endure hardness. That word endure means to accept or survive. Endure means not giving in to the pressures that have been heaped upon you. [All right.] Endure means to persevere in spite of the odds. Endurers are persecuted and endurers are made to go in lion's dens, fiery furnaces. Endurers are placed on islands of Patmos, on crosses. [Lord God.] Endurers have a hard fight, and if we're going to be in this warfare of God we much have that kind of endurance that will not lie down and give in to things. [All right now.] For the path of righteousness is one of hardness, and this hardness meets all of us in every facet and phase of our existence. No wonder he said, "Thou therefore endure harness, as a good soldier." [Well, well.]

At the time of this text dark was the plight of the Christian faith. Paul the apostle was aware of the great price Christians were paying at that time just to keep the faith. For ever since the church had been established it had had a bloody, bloody history. Some of God's people had been thrown in dens where hungry lions waited for them. Some had been made spectators, so as to be thrust into amphitheaters and made to fight like gladiators. Some of God's people had been put bound into overpopulated jails. Many prayer meetings had been disrupted by Roman soldiers because it was a federal offense to be caught having a Christian prayer meeting. The apostle Paul had seen the wrist and ankles of God's people bound with chains and shackles, all because they called the name Jesus.

Paul himself had heard the whack of the ax at Nero's chopping block and had seen the Roman soldiers gather up the heads of the saints like they were souvenirs. And I hear him saying to his spiritual son Timothy, "I'm in jail now, son, wish I could be there with you, but don't surrender; don't succumb. Son, don't give up. Thou therefore endure hardness, as a good soldier." [All right.]

Notice if you please, that he uses the terminology "good soldier." Paul does not say endure as a soldier, because all soldiers are not necessarily "good" soldiers. [All right. Say that.] Some soldiers need nothing but a mere temptation and they become cowards, idle, useless, and worthless. But the good soldier is bravest of the brave and more courageous than all. "Thou therefore endure hardness, as a good soldier."

The question which arises at this time is what are some of the traits and attributes and characteristics of a good soldier? Well, the first thing about a good soldier is that a good soldier is one who believes in the cause for which he fights. As Dr. Franklin would say,

"As my mind takes a stroll back down memory lane," and I reminisce the decades of the 60s, I bring into mental focus a man Cassius Clay, alias Mohammed Ali. When the U.S. Army was involved in a war in Vietnam, they called Cassius Clay to come to war. But he raised himself up as what they called a conscientious objector, told the whole wide world that the U.S. government was wrong for having involved itself in the political war of Vietnam. Cassius made everybody to know that even if they made him go to the battlefield that he would refuse to fight because he did not believe in the cause.

As we stop this afternoon and think upon the cause of Christians and all that is at stake in that cause—it's the kingdom of God that is at stake—the crown of Jesus—the cross, the gospel—the doctrines of truth, all of these are at stake and if we are going to be a good soldier, we must first of all believe in the cause! [Amen. That's right.]

In other words you've got to believe in the preaching of the gospel. [Well.] You've got to believe in prayer. You've got to believe in the Bible. You've got to believe in giving tithes. You've got to believe in heaven. You've got to believe in hell. You've got to believe in right. You've got to believe in wrong. You've got to believe in being born again. You've got to believe in doing unto others as you would have them do unto you. You've got to believe in working out your soul salvation in trembling and in fear. You have GOT to believe! [Amen. Yeah, That's right.]

All of us in this room today I'm sure will attest with me when I say that Dr. C.L. Franklin believed. It is utterly impossible for any man to have preached and taught the gospel as he did and not believe in that gospel. [Amen. That's right.] That's why I can say he was a good soldier. Paul said, Thou therefore endure hardness, as a good soldier."

Another thing about a good soldier is that he deeps in contact with the commander in chief. In the army the breakdown is that the private takes his orders from the corporal. The corporal takes his orders from the sergeant. The sergeant takes his orders from the lieutenant. The lieutenant takes his orders from the captain and on up the line. But, all of them at some time or another have to make contact with the commander in chief. [Amen.]

In God's army, Jesus Christ is the commander in chief. [All right. Come on now.] Gabriel, Raphael, and Michael and the other archangels are the five-star generals. The forty-eight angels are the generals. The twenty-four elders are the colonels. The patriarchs are the majors. The prophets are the captains. [Say on.] The saints are the lieutenants. The preachers of the gospel are the corporals, and every child of God on this smoky battlefield is a private who's trying to serve this present age [Amen.], his calling to fulfill! [That's it. Say it. Wooh. Yeah.] I'm talking today about a good soldier. [Amen. All right.]

When a soldier goes down to enlist in the army, that soldier first must be drilled and trained because a good soldier does not become good overnight. A lot of pain and anguish he must go through. Many hours of work and dedication me must endure. It's not an easy job to be a good soldier.

When that soldier enters basic training there are three things he's taught. He is taught number one to obey orders. Secondly he's taught how to put on his uniform and use his weapon. Thirdly, he's taught self-sacrifice. A good soldier is one who works around the clock. He does not go after his own pleasure, because he lives under the law and rule of another. A good soldier does not indulge in moonlighting—run no business on the side. A good soldier, even when he's asleep and not on call, is till supposed to be on duty. He's not concerned about his own wishes and his own whims, but he moves at the word of his commander. Whatever the commander tells him to do, that's what he does. If the commander tells him, "Get up," he gets up. If the commander tells him, "Fall in," he falls in. [All right. Go ahead.] If the commander tells him, "Attention," he puts both feet together, chest out, shoulders back. If the commander tells him, "At ease," he relaxes. If the commander says, "Fall out," he falls out. A good soldier obeys the commands of the chief officer.

As I stop and let my mind go back over the ministry of Dr. Franklin, all of us in this room today must again agree that he was obviously a good soldier. He obeyed orders. [Amen. Yes] One day there came the command to him, go ye therefore unto all the world and preach the gospel. You know and I know he did go. You know and I know he did preach. He obeyed orders because, ahah, he was a good soldier. [Amen. That's right.]

Then a good soldier, brothers and sisters, wears his uniform. Oh, when he's at ease he may enjoy putting on his warfare finery. But when it comes down to real warfare, he's not concerned about the brass and the buttons. The smoke and the dust and the garments of blood are tolled up on the battlefield. The sword, the bruised armor, the dented shields, these are things that mark a good soldier and causes one to go asoldiering.

We who fight the Christian fight, we too have our uniform. Paul told us in Ephesians the sixth chapter, verses eleven through fifteen, that we too have our uniform, for he says, "Put on the whole armor of God, that ye may be able to stand against the wiles of the devil" (KJV). Let me tell you one thing, church, we are not wrestling against a common, ordinary, everyday enemy, for he goes on to tell us that we're wrestling against principalities, against powers, against the rulers of darkness of this world, against spiritual wickedness in high places. Put on, I said, the "whooollllle" armor of God.

Then in that fourteenth verse, he starts listing the different pieces of the uniform. Funny he starts with girdle up your loins in truth. I used to wonder why he started there and didn't start with the hands or the feet, but said girdle up the loins with truth. You see those Roman soldiers wore short skirts. Those short skirts were very much like the Scottish kilts. Over those skirts they had their tunic or long cloak, and whenever that soldier would get into war he would first pull up that tunic and tuck it under his girdle so that his legs would be free, so that his feet would be unimpeded and he could adequately do battle. Oh you understand me. When ever you'd see a soldier with his loins girded, you knew then that he was ready for war.

In like manner if we're going to fight the Christian fight, we must gird ourselves in truth. Then we must, he said, put on the breastplate of righteousness. That breastplate they wore covered and protected their hearts, lungs, and other vital organs that were contained therein. The breastplate of righteousness protects us in that it provides us with a good conscience that protects us from malice, envy, jealousy, and strife, frees men from the terrors and evils of the world.

Then I heard him say, "Put on your feet the shoes of the gospel." Your feet got to be shod with the gospel of peace. Ahh, you're not complete as a soldier if you don't put on your gospel shoes—the shoes of peace. Can you imagine a supposed-to-be soldier, with his helmet on his head, breastplate across his chest, shield on his arm, sword in his hand, and still has no shoes on his feet? [Say it.] No matter how complete his uniform is, he is incomplete if he has no shoes on his feet. [Come on up. All right.] Sharp rocks and stones will bruise and cut his feet. To make his wardrobe complete, he must shod his feet with the gospel of peace.

Then I heard him say put the shield of faith on your arm. I hear somebody say if there's ever a piece of a soldier's uniform one needs to have, it is the shield of faith. [All right. Then say it.]

Ahh, you can still fight a good fight if you have no breastplate of righteousness. You can fight a good fight if you have no gospel of peace on your feet. You can still fight if you don't have a helmet. If you've got to pick one thing, it's best to pick the shield of faith because that shield protects you from the fiery darts of the evil one. [Amen.]

I hear somebody say well, if that's all I really need, why put on the breastplate, shoes, the helmet? The answer comes back, the Bible says we are not only called upon to be conquerors but we are to be more than conquerors. [Amen. Say it.] We must not only win, but we must win abundantly, triumphantly, victoriously.

Oh, he goes on to say, "Put the helmet of salvation on your head," which means that you are saved. Saved, preacher? Yes, saved. Saved from the fresh inroads of sin. Saved from the stain of death. Saved from the victory of the grave. Saved from unholy influences. Saved from evil impulses. Put on, I say, the helmet of salvation!

Then if you're going to be in my army, you must take up the sword of the spirit. That spirit is nothing but the Word of God. God's Word you know is supernatural in origin, divine in authorship [Yeah, say it.], human in penmanship [Come on. Say it.], infallible in authority, infinite in scope, universal in interest [Watch it.], personal in application [Yeah], positive in declaration, wonderful in its translation, in its inspiration, and in its declaration of the final consummation. Pick up, I said, the SWORD of the spirit. [Wooh. Say it.]

Tell you what I want you to notice though. Notice I got the helmet of salvation on my head. Notice I got the breast plate of righteousness on my chest. [Yeah. Come on up.] Notice I got my loins girded and my body. [Yes. Say it now. Come on.] Notice I got the gospel of peace on my feet. [Yes sir.] I got the shield of faith on my arm and the sword of the spirit in my hand. [Yeah.] With all the soldier has, even a breastplate, there's nothing on his back. [All right preacher. My Lord.] Somebody says why is it that a soldier does not have a backplate? The reason why is a soldier is always going somewhere, always pressing ahead, never can turn around. [Yeah. Say it.] If he turns around then the old devil may shoot him down.

As I think about Dr. Franklin, he too had no backplate; he was always pressing on. I heard him say, "I'm pressing on [Say it.] the upward way. New heights I'm gaining every day." Because he knew what the Bible said in Revelation 2 verse 10, "Be thou faithful unto death, and I will give you a crown of life." [Oh yeah. He's going up.] He did not say be thou faithful until death, and I don't know the reason we somehow falsely use that verse and somehow we misquote that valuable verse in our Bible. [That's right. Take us up.] My God, it does not say, be thou faithful until death. My God, rather it says, be thou faithful unto death. And there is a difference in the word until and the word unto. [Yes. Say it.] Oh Lawddd. [Say it. That's it.]

The word until means to a certain point. But the word unto means beyond the point. [Yeah. Say it. Come on up.] Ahh Lawd. Anah', until means it's limited [Yeah.], but the word unto means beyond all bounds and beyond all limits; ahhh Lawd. [Yes.]

Anah' as I think about this church, ahh Lawd, and how Dr. Franklin brought this church from a might long ways [Yeah.]; ahh Lawd, evidence shows, uhhum, evidence shows that he had too many until members instead of unto members [Yeah. Say it.], ahh Lawd. And, he had some "Reverend Franklin I with yah, until I disagree with yah," members [Say it. Tell the truth.]; aah' Lawd. And, Dr. Franklin until you hurt my feelings and I'm with yah, until you don't call my name.

That's why I'm glad the writer did not say, "be faithful until." But, I hear him saying, "Be faithful unto death." [Preach. Preach.] Anah,' ohhhh Lawd, and the road may be rough and the going may be tough, ummhm'. [Say it.] But I hear him saying, "Don't be faithful until bad things happen, but be faithful unto death." [Yes.] Yesssss. That means until death comes. So I hear him saying, ooohh Lawd, be thou faithful unto death, and I will give thee then a crown of life, ooohhh yes. Ahh yes.

Anah' I'm gonna close here [Well. Say it. Yeah.] when I tell you just one more thing. It is said that back during the days of the Civil War, when the North and the South were at war, one with another. [Yes.] Anah' you know how our forefathers yearned and burned and prayed to be free. Anah' after awhile many of them learned that the Union army was one their way. [Yeah. Tell it.] Anah' there was an old black man on this plantation that was born in slavery. Anah' when he heard that the Union army was on its way he got him some sticks and got him some rocks and started down to the battlefield, ahh yes. [Yes. Take us up.]

And somebody said, "John, where are you going with stones and sticks?" I heard him say, "I'm going down to the battlefield to help the Union army win this battle." But then, someway and somehow, yesssss, John was shot down on that battlefield. Anah', one of his friends walked up to him and held him in his arms, and I heard him say, "If my relatives ask you how I died, if my friends should ask you how I died, well, tell them I died on the field." [Yeah. Say it.] Oh yessss. You see, the Lord does not want us to rust out, but God wants us to wear out. Oh yessss. Dr. Franklin you know was still on the field.

I'm gone let you alone now. But I hear somebody saying, well Jasper, you told us about a good soldier. I heard you say that a good soldier obeys orders. I heard you say that a good soldier learns how to put on his uniform and how to use his weapon. I hear you say that a good soldier is self-sacrificing. Anah', but Jasper, tell me, is that it? Is there anything else you've got to say about a good soldier? Oh Lawwd. Yessss, there's one more thing I've got to tell you. [Yeah. Yes. Say it. Lord. Oh Lord. Say it, preacher.]

Did you hear what I said, there's one moooore thing I got to tell yah. Yes, a good soldier stays until he receives orders to come on home. [Yeah. Yes. Say it. Wooh.] Do you hear what I'm sayin'? He may be wounded on the battlefield [Yeah. Yes.], but though he's wounded, he['s gotta stay there, yes, uhuh, uhhuum, stay there, until he get orders to come on home. Oh yes he does.

More than five years ago, Dr. Franklin got wounded on the battlefield. He went by home to get his clothes to be here on this battlefield that Sunday morning. [Yeah. Yes. Oh yeah. Say it.] He was shot and wounded on the battlefield, but he stayed right there; ahh y'all don't hear me. [Yes. Say it. Lord God.] But he stayed right there. He stayed there [Yes. He did. Yeah.], stayed there, five long years, but the other Friday morning [Yeah preacher.] he got his orders, yeahhh, ahhhhhh come on home; ahhhhhh come on home.

I'm gon' leave when I'll tell you, I'm on the battlefield for my Lord. [Say it.] Do you hear what I'm saying? [Yes. Say it. Yeah preacher.]

I promised him that I [Yeah. Wooh. Say it.] would serve him, servvvve himmmmm, serrrrrve him until I die. Yes. [Yes. Ah yes.] Yes. [Yes.] Yessssss, ahhhhhh yes. [Yes. Say it. Wooh. My Lord. Oh Lord. Say it.]

When I get down to my last hour, I want my wife to say [Yeah. Say it. Yeah.] I've been a good husband. [Yes. Yeah.] I want my children to say I've been a good father. I want my members to say [Yeah. Yes.] I've been a sho'-nuff good pastor. [Yeah. Say it.] I want people to say I've been a good preacher. [Say it. We hear ya.] But most of all, do you hear what I'm saying, I want the Lord to say, ahhhhhhhhhh-hh good soldier, ahhhhhhhhhh good soldier, ahh you don't hear me, ahhhhhhhhhh.

He was a good soldier. I feel all right today. I'm glad to be here where I'm standing. I'm glad I've got the last word to say about a good soldier; ahhhhhhhhhh, he finished. I hear him sayin' I've fought hell and sin. Yeahhhhhhh I fought; he finished y'all hear—y'all hear what I'm saying? He finished his course and he kept the faith. I hear God saying, to him servant, ahhhhhhhhhh servant, ahh-hhhhhhhh servant, can I say it just one more time? [Yeah. Yeah.] Well done, well done, well done, ahhhhhhhhhh, well done. [Applause.]

I hear Doc sayin,

[Preacher begins to sing in the style of a long-meter hymn]

If I don't wake up in the morning everything is all right. If I don't wake up in the morning, everything is all right, ahhhhhhhhh right.

[Then preacher sings:]

I've got a few more tears to shed.

I've got a few more burden to bear.

I've got a few more times to give up the right for the wrong.

Ahhhhhhhhhh, I'm gonna keep on, till the battle has been fought, and victory has been won. If you get to heaven before I do, save a seat for me.

The Road that Leads to Wholeness

W. FRANKLYN RICHARDSON II

I n "The Road That Leads to Wholeness," W. Franklyn Richardson
once again conveys a timeless message to his audience. He
addresses those who are "broken," who face "the pain of loneliness
and of separation." Many, he observes, are cleansed, but not whole,
and he reminds us of the healing and wholeness that can only be
found in grace, in God.

The Road that Leads to Wholeness

I want to solicit your attention to a passage of scripture that is centered in the experience of ten men. Even though the main characters are men, this story applies to both men and women. This word is found in the seventeenth chapter of the Gospel according to Luke, starting at the eleventh verse:

> And it came to pass, as he went to Jerusalem, that he
> passed though the midst of Samaria and Galilee. And
> as he entered into a certain village, there met him ten
> men that where lepers, which stood afar off: And they
> lifted up their voices, and said, Jesus, Master, have
> mercy on us. And when he saw them, he said unto
> them, Go show yourselves unto the priests. And it came
> to pass, that, as they went, they were cleansed. And one
> of them, when he saw that he was healed, turned back,
> and with a loud voice glorified God. And fell down on
> his face at his feet, giving him thanks: and he was a
> Samaritan. And Jesus answering said, were there not

ten cleansed? but where are the nine? There are not found that returned to give glory to God, save this stranger? And he said unto him, Arise, go thy way: thy faith hath made thee whole

LUKE 17:11-19 KJV

I want to talk today from the subject, "The Road That Leads To Wholeness;" w-h-o-l-e-n-e-s-s. "The Road That Leads To Wholeness." Now, this title makes no sense unless the person who hears it has come to grips with the fact that they are broken and less than whole. In fact, this lecture will not interest you unless you understand that you are indeed broken—less than whole, and, in need of healing. This is not an important announcement for those of us who think we've already got everything together. But, for those of us who KNOW that we are broken, that we are not what we ought to be, this announcement has implications for the rest of our lives. "The Road That Leads To Wholeness."

Now, everybody, no matter who we are, if we are in our right minds and of sound spirit, we want to be whole. At some time in our lives, we come face to face with the longing to be all that God intends for us to be. We want to be what God had in mind, when, on the morning of creation, God spoke humankind into existence. We want to be whole. And the truth of the matter is that none of us is even born whole. We don't come into the world whole. It is a part of the contract of our humanity.

Every since humanity fell in the Garden of Eden by disobeying God, people have been born with an intrinsic brokeness. Which is to say that God's vision of us has been distorted by our disobedience. So it is that we all come limping into the world. We do not walk with the stride of eternity's morning, but, we walk, like Jacob, with a limp. We're not whole. However, God did not leave it so that we could not become whole again. We are not left forever with this limp. Our brokeness can be bound. My inadequacies can be overcome. I can be what God intended for me to be.

This passage is about ten men who are broken; ten men who have a dreaded disease which is believed to be infectious—leprosy. Leprosy attacks the skin, flesh and nerves. A leper is subject to breaking out with nodules, ulcers, and white, scaly scabs. And, because it wastes the body, deformity is a progressive outcome of this disease. The sufferer looses limbs and has running sores full of pus. The disease was thought to be extremely contagious. They're broken. They're less than what God intended them to be. They are diseased.

I want you to see them now. They are ten men who have a disease that there is no cure for. No penicillin. No doctor. No clinic. They have a disease that has caused them to be ostracized and cut off from everybody else; a disease that has put them on the fringes of the community; a disease that has taken away their home life and destroyed their ability to work. NOBODY WANTS TO BE AROUND A LEPER; NOT EVEN A WIFE; NOT EVEN A CHILD. Therefore, lepers were made to live in a community of leperous persons.

I want you to see it. They're been put out of church because they've got leprosy. They've lost everything and they live in a ghetto of leperous persons, dwelling on the outskirts of the town, because they've got leprosy. The have nothing to live for. Their hope has been shattered. They're walking along, but, there is no enthusiasm in their stride. There is no brightness in their faces. They just drag along, with no cadence to their step.

They have no where to go and no time to be there. Their heads are bowed and there is on their faces the pain of loneliness and of separation. Their arms are limp. Their backs are bent. They are just walking along. They don't have anywhere to go. They have no hope that they will ever get better. There is no doctor for them to go to. They are just walking along.

They've lost everything—no family, no friends. The only people they can look at are other folks who have leprosy like them. They're hopelessly locked out from the rest of society and desperately locked into their lepers' ghetto. They are afraid to hope for a cure. Even so, they yearn to live among other folks again. They long for the bosom of their families.

They had no hope, and no neighbors who were not also lepers like themselves. The Jews had a law that no one was to come within fifteen feet of a leper. No one was to get near them because leprosy was thought to be contagious. The disease might be brought back to the city if lepers were allowed in. But, somebody got close enough to them to tell those ten men some GOOD NEWS. Somebody got close enough to whisper to them, "THERE'S A MAN IN TOWN." Oh glory hallelujah! "There's a man in town."

You know, that all I heard. That's all somebody told me one day. And, if you've been saved, that's what you heard. You heard, "There's a man in town." Somebody told them, "There's a man in town." They said, "He heals the sick and he gives sight to the blind." There's a man in town. "He met a woman at Jacob's well, a prostitute; sent her back a missionary." There's a man in town. "He stopped at the cemetery four days after the funeral and called the dead man from the grave. Told the mourners to loosen him and let him go." There's a man in town. "He stepped out of the Galilean Sea and spoke to the cosmic elements; told the wind to stop blowing and the waves to lay down." There's a man in town. "He took sand and put in on a blind man's eye." There's a man in town!!

When they heard this word of hope, their backs began to straighten. Can't you see them? Can you hear how they talk with new enthusiasm; can't you see how their steps have new definition? How smiles begin to radiate across their faces? They are STILL sick, but, the fact is, now they have the hope that they may get well. Sometimes the hope of getting well is just as good as getting well.

They get excited and they decide to go out on the outskirts of the city and wait for Jesus. They've heard about him and they say to themselves that each other, "Maybe he can help us. Maybe he can deal with this brokeness that keeps us from being all that we can be." And so, they wait on the outside of the city. They are like a reception committee. They're waiting there for Jesus. After a while, Jesus comes by and they cry out, "Lord, have mercy, have mercy on us!" Oh, there is a whole lot of preaching in that.

Notice that the lepers don't say "Lord, get rid of this leprosy." I think that as Christians, people who pray, we would do well to somehow learn how to incorporate into our prayer style the ability to say "Have mercy Lord." So many of us want to tell God what to do, what time to do it, and how to do it, but, mature faith knows how to say "Lord, have mercy." The ten lepers don't say "Lord, take away this leprosy." They just say, "Have mercy."

We need to learn how to say "Have mercy." We need to learn how to say "Have mercy" because to do so is to acknowledge the sovereignty of God. Further, to ask for God's mercy, expecting to rely on it, is a great statement of faith. It acknowledges that God already knows what you're going through and that God knows how to bring you through what you are going through.

You know sometimes we ought to say "Have Mercy" because we really don't know how to ask for what we need. Sometimes the thing we want to get rid of is the very thing the Lord has sent to give us our blessing. Sometimes our burdens bring us our blessings. Blessings don't always come on flowery beds of ease. Sometimes blessings come through the storm and the rain, sometimes through the storms and pain.

I remember that, early on in my ministry, there was a church that I pastured where it seems that, no matter what I'd do, there was a group of folks who didn't like me. I'd pray and they didn't like me. I'd preach and sing, and they didn't like me. When they'd get sick,

I'd run to go see them first and they didn't like me. It seems that I could't do anything to win those folks so that we could come together to do the work of the Lord.

One day I found myself going down on my knees and talking to God about it. I remember earnestly saying, "Lord, I wish that you would take these folks out of my way." I said, "Lord, let them go to another church or something. Lord, I've tried and I can't seem to win them. I can't seem to move them by my witness." And I remember finishing my prayers, and, before I could get up off of my knees, the Lord answered me. It seemed to me that God said, "You leave them alone." God said, "I sent them there and they're there to make you a better preacher. If they weren't there, you wouldn't be the kind of preacher you are. If they weren't there you wouldn't know how to get on your knees." Oh glory! Sometimes the thing we want to get rid of is the thing the Lord has sent us to show us how to be stronger Christians. I learned how to pray because of those hard-hearted, cantankerous people. God didn't have to move that stumbling block. The Lord just gave me the room to go around it. God doesn't have to move the mountain to give us the strength to climb it. The lepers wait for Jesus, and, when he comes to the outskirts of town, they say, "Lord, have mercy." Jesus says to them, "Go show yourselves to the priests."

Now you need to know that during this particular period in human history, among the Jews, if, by some miracle, you were delivered from leprosy, you had to go up to the synagogue and have the priest perform a ritual which announced to the city that you were now ceremonially clean. Only then would you be allowed back into the city.

Now, when Jesus says to them, "Go show yourselves to the priests," it is either an insane statement, or, a statement meant to solicit their faith. For, you see, when Jesus tells the ten lepers to "go show yourselves to the priests," they still have leprosy. They still have pus running from their sores. When Jesus says "go show yourselves to the priests," they are still shackled with their brokeness. They are still victimized by their society because they are lepers. Here Jesus is saying, "Go show yourselves to the priests," and they are still lepers. They are still sick. Well now, if some of us had been there, we probably would have said, "Well now Lord, I WOULD go up there to the priests, but I've still got this leprosy, and there is no need for me to go to the temple yet! When I get there the priests are just going to send me back, because I HAVE STILL GOT IT!!! As a matter of fact, I might be stoned to death. The Law says to stone anyone who breaks the covenant rules for the safety of the community. You KNOW that Lord."

But, the ten lepers don't say any of that. The Bible says that, when Jesus tells them to go, "AS THEY WENT, THEY WERE HEALED." When they started out on the journey to the priests, they still had leprosy. They hadn't been cured when they started out.

It's that way MOST of the time when we start out in faith; we can't see the end result. When we start out in faith we can't see what the end is going to be. We can't see how it's going to end up with we're working with God. Oh, sometimes I wish that I COULD see how it's going to end, but, when you go for God, you've got to go on faith. Sometimes everything around you and everybody around you, suggests defeat. Sometimes all you've got is God's word. Sometimes all you have is God's word and God's promise. And God's promise is often in conflict with what you see going on, but, it's all you've got. And what is God's promise? God has promised that, "if you go child, I'll go with you. I'll be with you, ALWAYS."

The Bible says that the ten lepers start going toward where the priests are ON THE STRENGTH OF JESUS' WORDS—BECAUSE he told them to. The Bible says, "as they went," as they did what God told them to do; as they said "yes" to the Lord, they were cleansed. As they were obedient to God's word their healing came down. In the process of obeying God, they were healed.

You see, on this Christian journey, we get cleansed ON OUR WAY. When Jesus calls us to "go" our Christian journey's have just begun. The call to "go" is just the beginning. You didn't get it all that morning when you got converted. You might have been converted twenty-five years ago, but, if you're the same kind of Christian today that you were twenty-five years ago, then, you didn't get anything when you got it. We meet the Lord, our cleansing comes as we go on the journey. As we say "yes" to the Lord, our cleaning comes.

These ten men were cleansed of their leprosy as they went; in the process of going to the priests. My grandfather, who was also a preacher, would have said it like this: "they looked at their hands and their hands looked new; they looked at their feet and they did too; they started walking and they had a new walk; started talking and they had a new talk."

That's the way it is when you meet Jesus. Every day with Jesus is sweeter than the day before, even though all you have is a promise. But, if you go on God's word God has promised to be with you. God has promised to make a way. God has promised to make you whole. If you go on the strength of Jesus' words, it may be dark and there may be storms in your life; the rain may come and the wind may blow, but, if you go on because he said so, if you are stayed on the word, then, in the process of saying "yes" your cleansing will come— in the very process of going where the Lord wants you to go; in the process of doing what the Lord want you to do.

The Bible says that the ten lepers were cleansed, and, when they go to the priests, they made them ceremonially right. They made their healing official in their community. But, the Bible reports something else of those men. Nine of them who belonged to the "better race," nine of them, who were outstanding because they were Hebrews; nine of them who had regained a place in society; nine of them who had a high vocation; none of them who had been blessed to return to their families; nine of them went on back to their homes and to their families, without another word to Jesus. But, one of them, who was a member of the "mongrel race; one of them, who was a second-class citizen; one of them who probably had no fine home to return to; one of them, who was a Samaritan, and hated by the Jews and only allowed with the others because they were all lepers; that one went back to where Jesus was. He went back to where the man was who had sent him to be healed. He went back and said, "Jesus, thank you. I had to come back. I had to acknowledge what you have done for me. You brought me from a mighty long way Lord, and, I cam back to say 'thank you.' I just came back to . . . say 'thank you.'"

Jesus looks up. "Where are the other nine that I cleansed? Didn't I heal ten of you?" The healed man says, "well, I guess they had other things to do. Maybe they had to get back to what they were doing before they got leprosy. They were really excited when they left the temple." Jesus says, "but you came back to say 'thank you?'" And then Jesus looks at him and says, "the others were only cleansed, but, your faith has made you whole."

You see, there are a whole lot of us in the Church who are clean. We look good on the outside. We've been cleansed. We've been in the Church a long time. We're clean. We've got lovely positions and we live in lovely homes. We're clean. We're deacons and preachers, trustees and choir members. We're clean, But, you cannot be whole until you understand that whatever you have is from the Lord. Whatever I have comes from the Lord. I can't be whole until I understand that I am what I am by the grace of God. We can't be whole until we know about grace. "Amazing grace, how sweet the sound, that saved a wretch like me. I once was lost, but, now, I'm found, was blind but now I see." We can't be whole until we go back and say "thank you! Lord you brought me from a mighty long ways and I came back to say thank you. I was down but you picked me up. I was out but you brought me in. I was in the darkness but you gave me light. I was lost but you found me—and I came back, I came back, I came back, I came back—to say thank you. Thank you."

Amen.

The Still Small Voice of Calm

FREDERICK BOYD WILLIAMS

As does Gardner C. Taylor in his "Living With Change," Frederick Boyd Williams addresses the upset and turbulence that can afflict our lives. In "The Still Small Voice of Calm," Williams, in the tradition of the learned preachers of African American history, deftly utilizes the story of Elijah to pave the path to calmness and provide solutions.

The Still Small Voice of Calm

A sermon by The Rev. Canon Frederick Boyd Williams, Rector, Church of the Intercession (Anglican/Episcopal), New York City at The Presbyterian Church, Rensselaerville, New York, 27 June 1999, 11:00 A.M.

INTRODUCTION

First, I greet you this morning in the name of our risen Savior and Lord, Jesus Christ. May his presence and joy be evident in our time together.

Secondly, I thank you for the invitation to share once again in this fellowship . . . though quite frankly, I thought I was "off the hook" for this year . . . but with Barbara Dudley leading the charge . . . (and Tom Littlefield offering assistance) well . . . it is good to be back.

I bring you greetings from your Anglican/Episcopal sisters and brothers at the Church of the Intercession in Harlem/Washington Heights, where since 1846; the Gospel of Jesus Christ, crucified, raised, and coming again in Judgment, has been proclaimed. Today, at mass, even as I speak, they are praying for us . . .

Please join me in prayer.

INVOCATION

"May only God's Word be spoken. May only God's Word be heard. In the precious name of Jesus we pray. Amen.

TRANSITION

You have chosen as the theme for this summer's preaching series: "THE LIFE OF SPIRIT IN TURBULENT TIMES". . .

This is a theme that points to the concern of the need for spiritual renewal in times of change. It is an issue that reflects the coming millennium, but also one that is timeless in importance . . .

As I wrestled with the question of "what can I say about that?" the sometimes (oftimes?) hectic nature of my own life was suddenly illuminated, and I resonated with the story of the prophet Elijah, deep in despair and in a cave, as described in I Kings 19:1-12; and I remembered his need: our need; in turbulent times, for the comfort and guidance of:

TITLE "The Still Small Voice of Calm"

THE STORY

If there was ever a turbulent person, who lived in turbulent times, the prophet Elijah is your man. Clearly one of the most colorful and outspoken men in history, his reputation and esteem among the people of the first book are exceeded only by Moses. A patriot as well as a prophet, Elijah saved his nation from the errors and excesses of King Ahab and Queen Jezebel by serving as the conscience of Israel. He turned his nation away from the practice of child sacrifice in the encounters with the priests of Baal on Mt. Carmel (I Kgs. 18), and because of his faithfulness to and zeal for the word of God, had to flee for his life.

Elijah's ministry had been a ministry of Miracles, Fire, and the Sword. The commentators note that, "he had shut the heavens, had been sustained by ravens, and by a jar of meal and cruet of oil that was never empty, had raised the dead, had called down fire from heaven, and had brought rain to the land."

Later Jewish tradition would say he never died, but ascended to heaven in a chariot of fire while still alive. That legend says that even today, he now roams the earth awaiting the time when he will usher in the Messiah.

Indeed, Rabbi Naomi Levy, in her book, To Begin Again, writes that, "keeping Elijah's memory alive has been a way to keep Jewish hope alive no matter where Jews settled, no matter whether they were persecuted or exiled, no matter whether they were hated or tortured, Elijah's memory . . . gave them the strength to carry on . . . it enabled the Jewish people to withstand centuries of exile and uncertainty". . . But that is a later Elijah, not the utterly dejected, discouraged, fearful and despairing man we read about today, in a cave on Mt. Horeb (I Kgs. 19). . . . Listen again to the conversation . . . . "And there he came to a cave, and lodged there; and behold, the word of the Lord came to him, and he said to him, "What are you doing here, Elijah?" He said, "I have been very jealous for the Lord, the God of hosts; for the people of Israel have forsaken thy covenant, thrown down thy altars, and slain thy prophets with the sword; and I, even I only, am left; and they seek my life, to take it away." (I Kgs 19:9-10) Elijah the turbulent was in a turbulent situation, and needed his faith renewed . . . and the God of Faith was not about to fail, even if the lesson to be learned, the gift to be received, was totally unexpected . . . .

. . . Listen again to the conversation . . . And he said, "Go forth, and stand upon the mount before the Lord." And behold, the Lord passed by, and a great and strong wind rent the mountains, and broke in pieces the rocks before the Lord, but the Lord was not in the wind; and after the wind an earthquake, but the Lord was not in the earthquake; and after the earthquake a fire, but the Lord was not in the fire; and after the fire a still small voice. (I Kgs 19:11-12) One author has written; "It seems like God was aiming to tell Elijah that, while force and spectacular demonstrations of power are sometimes necessary by reason of crisis in God's plans, yet after all, God's real work in the world is not accomplished by such methods; that God sometimes does and sometimes calls men and women to do things that are utterly contrary to God's nature to do."

. . . Listen again to the conversation . . . And when Elijah heard it, he wrapped his face in his mantle and went out and stood at the entrance of the cave. And behold, there came a voice to him, and said, "What are you doing here, Elijah?" He said, "I have been very jealous for the Lord, the God of hosts; for the people of Israel have forsaken thy covenant, thrown down thy altars, and slain thy prophets with the sword; and, I, even I only, am left; and they seek my life, to take it away." And the Lord said to him, "Go, return on your way to the wilderness of Damascus; and when you arrive, you shall anoint Hazel to be the king over Syria; and Jehu the son of Nimshi you shall anoint to be king over Israel; and Eli'sha the son of Shaphat of Abelmeholah you shall anoint to be prophet in your place. And him who escapes from the sword of Hazel shall Jehu slay; and him who escapes from the sword of Jehu shall Eli'sha slay. Yet will leave seven thousand in Israel, all the knees that have not bowed to Ba'al, and every mouth that has not kissed him." So he departed from there, and found Eli'sha the son of Shaphat, who was plowing, with twelve yoke of oxen before him, and he was with the twelfth. Eli'jah passed by him and cast his mantle upon him. (I KGS 19:13-19)

On church! In a turbulent time, God Touched the spirit of Elijah, lifted him up and sent him back to serve the people!

In that turbulent time, God renewed Elijah in such a manner so he could pass on his zeal for justice and obedience to God to all who would follow in his footsteps!

In that turbulent time, Eli'jah now understood that he was being sent back to renew the struggle by a God who knew no defeat!

In that turbulent time, Eli'jah no longer felt alone. He was confident that God would make good God's cause, and so Eli'jah became resolute and effective in his ministry . . . .as I KGS 18:37

"He so brought the people's heart back again to God," that even Jezebel gave up her wicked ways. . .

TWO questions:

THE TEACHING

The 1st Question: How and why did this renewal of Elijah's Spirit occur? The Scriptures recount a story in which at least five dynamics are revealed, and are therefore useful for our own search for renewal.

1. Elijah was faithful to the traditions of his people, i.e.: He did not forget "the rock from which he was hewn, nor the pit from which he was dug." when trouble came, even in his despair, he remembered the places where God had met his people. In the hour of his deepest discouragement, he fled to that Holy place in search of God (as we sing in "Lift Every Voice," stz. 3). God of our weary years, God of our silent tears, Thou who has brought us thus far on the way. Thou who hast by thy might, led us into the light, Keep us forever in the path, we pray. Lest our feet stray from the places, our God, where we met thee, Lest our hearts, drunk with the wine of the world, we forget thee, Shadowed beneath Thy hand, May we forever stand, True to our God, true our native land.

2. Elijah remembered that there is only one True God. In the words of Soren Kirkegaard, he knew "that purity of heart is to will one thing." That the Lord God of Israel would not share His glory or reverence with any other.

3. Elijah learned that God never gives up on us. Even when we give up on ourselves. Our God is an Intervener, a "doing" God, the God with a plan summoning His faithful servants to carry that plan out in and against the desires of the world.

4. Elijah experienced God as the one who Loves his people. No matter how far we stray from God's presence and will, God's desire for us is to bring us to a better mind so we can receive God's blessing.

5. Elijah in his moment of despair finally learned the true power of prayer. He learned to "stand" before God, "face to face," and let "God be God;" not as we chose, not as we expect, not as we imagine, but simply as God decides when and how to reveal himself to those he chooses, then for us to accept that revelation and respond in obedience and faithfulness.

Examples: Mary at the annunciation ("behold the handmaid . . .") Jesus in the Garden ("not my will but thine . . .") Thomas in the Upper Room ("My Lord and my God . . .")

The 2nd Question: What keels us today from hearing and learning as Elijah did? There are many factors one could cite, but here are three from the wisdom of my Cherokee ancestors, who also knew and experienced the comfort and guidance of the "Still, Small Voice of Calm."

THREE BARRIERS TO BE OVERCOME

1. Habit and "Blindness"

Habit so dulls the edge of observation that it is easy to a pass a tree and never see its beautiful seasons—or be around another person for a lifetime and never see the beauty of the soul. We travel great distances to see something beautiful, and go to great lengths to get a glimpse of a famous person—but our immediate surroundings fade so easily. Familiar faces, voices, the easy touch of hands—are all taken for granted. With a firm foundation they can be relaxed and confident, but we still need to stay alert to their importance. Even good habits can dull our awareness to things necessary and dear to us."

TEN BEARS

2. Quiet Moments & "Big Decisions"

"Chances are we never recall just when we made the biggest decision in our lives—unless we can remember some of our quietest moments. We think of change coming with fanfare, but that so seldom happens. Most of the time we silently recognize the great things in our lives long before we bring them out to be known by everyone. It is hard to say just when the change began. Some of it is even sacred to us, not easily shared-not wise to share, because it is our own that comes from somewhere deep within us. There is an inner life that makes changes easier because it prepares us to accept what we cannot change—and more importantly, to change what we can."

WOVOKA

3. The Role of Silence

"Talking too much is a little like painting a picture. It is frequently what we leave out that makes it the masterpiece. We don't have to tell everything we think—nor use every color on the palette. Subtlety makes someone else think, and that is more important. Our tendency is to think that no one understands unless we spell things out for them. It is hard to keep our mouths shut when we want to say something so much—usually with an irony or a degree of sarcasm, according to the Cherokee. Silence can be as unkind as saying too much but in the long run it serves a better purpose in preserving friendships. There is a time to speak and a time to keep silence, but it is a person of rare sensitivity who knows when the time is."

INDIAN COUNCIL

Habit and Blindness
Quiet moments and Big decisions
Understanding the Role of Silence

Three Barriers to Overcome . . . .
Q: "What are you doing here Elijah?"
A: "Lord, I seek to renew my spirit in these troubled times!"
God's Response: "Arise. Do not be afraid. Return to the people. I
have work for you to do."

I leave you with a song from my childhood in Tennessee: "He knows
Just How Much We Can Bear."

> We are our heavenly Father's Children
> And we all know that He loves us one and all;
> Yet there are times when we find we answer,
> Another's voice and call;
> If we are willing, He will teach us,
> His voice only to obey no matter where,
> and He knows, Yes, He knows,
> Just how much we can bear.

> Refrain
> Tho' the load gets heavy,
> You're never left alone to bear it all;
> Ask for the Strength and keep on toiling,
> tho' the tear-drops fall.
> You have the joy of this assurance:
> The heavenly Father will always answer prayer,
> and He knows, Yes, He knows
> Just how much we can bear.

God bless you, as you discover for yourself—"The Still Small Voice
of Calm."

Tributes to Genius:
Eulogy of Howard Thurman

LERONE BENNETT, JR., JESSE L. JACKSON
AND VERNON E. JORDAN, JR.

During the 1970s, Life magazine called Howard Thurman one of twelve "great preachers of the twentieth century." A minister and professor of religion, Thurman was one of the spiritual leaders of the civil rights movement of the 1960s. In 1981, his death called forth stirring tributes from many, including writer Lerone Bennett Jr., executive editor of Ebony magazine; minister and civil rights leader, Jesse L. Jackson; and statesman/lawyer Vernon E. Jordan Jr., former executive director of the National Urban League and former director of the United Negro College Fund.

Tributes to Genius:
Eulogy of Howard Thurman

LERONE BENNETT, JR.

And, when he shall die,
Take him and cut him out in little stars,
And he will make the face of heaven so fine
That all the world will be in love with night
And pay no worship to the garish sun[1]

The words are Shakespeare's, and they are arguably extravagant. But our duty here is to tell the truth about "the luminous darkness" of a rare and extravagant spirit who assumed the name Howard Thurman and walked with us for a little while on this earth.

It was an honor to live in the same world with this man. A poet, philosopher, seer, a great and gushing river of the spirit, he was an American original and one of the most gifted and creative thinkers of our times.

---

1. Shakespeare, William. Romeo and Juliet. Act 3, Scene 2.

"The only witness a man can make," he said to me once, subtly cautioning me against my wild flights into theory, "is the witness of his own experience."

Let me take him seriously here and say that I knew him as a friend and spiritual guidepost and that it is my personal testimony that he not only quoted Scripture but was a scripture. Gloria and I and our children had the honor of warming ourselves in the fire of his spirit, and we broke bread and laughed—was there ever a man, was there ever a preacher, who laughed with more contagion and joy?—with him and his golden companion of the years, Sue Bailey Thurman.

> Sunshine was he,
> In the winter day;
> And in the midsummer
> Coolness and shade

I knew him, then, as a friend, but I knew him also as a historical presence. And it is my witness as a historian that he was one of the true pioneers of nonviolence in this country and that his classic [book], Jesus and the Disinherited, is perhaps the best systematic exposition of that philosophy in a Christian context. I know personally that he was a great influence on Martin Luther King Jr., and when I went to Montgomery shortly after the beginning of the bus boycott, I was not al all surprised to find King reading not Gandhi but Howard Thurman.

Beyond all that, deeper than that, I knew Howard Thurman as a black man—a black man totally, passionately, creatively engaged in a quest for common ground beyond race, beyond creed, beyond labels. I knew him, in short, as a world soul, but the world soul I knew was a black world soul rooted in the universality of his own idiom, to use his word. "A man cannot be at home everywhere," he used to say, "unless he is at home somewhere." Howard Thurman was at home, and on the foundation of his at-homeness he created great gothic spires of the spirit that reached out to everything and everybody. And his true significance, I think, is in the fact that so many men and women of all races and creeds—blacks and whites, Jews and Gentiles, Hindus and Buddhists—found bread for their spirit in a made-in-America theology honed to a fine edge, not by a mystic from the East but by a grandson of slaves who came out of the black religious tradition with a message of hope and wholeness for all men, all women, all people.

It has been noted in the last few days that American media don't seem to know what an extraordinary spiritual phenomenon he was. But that's understandable. The media of Rome didn't know who Jesus was. The media of Germany didn't know who Bach was. The media of England didn't know who Shakespeare was. It is not at all surprising therefore that American media have not recognized the true importance of Howard Thurman. But when historians come, a hundred years from today, to set down the names of men and women in our times who served Jesus and the disinherited best, the name of Howard Thurman will be at or near the top.

I had the enormous honor of introducing him in several places, and I always embarrassed him. I can see him now, out of the corner of my eye, covering his face with his hands and trying to hide from the words of praise. He accused me once of saying in *Ebony* that he was a saint. That's not what I said, really. What I said then, and what I say now, is that he was either a saint or the closest thing to a saint that we are likely to see.

May Jehovah and Allah and Damballa and all the gods of our fathers and mothers make us worthy of him.

> He was here; now he is everywhere.
> He was part of our lives;
> Now he is part of all that ever was and
> All that ever will be.

JESSE L. JACKSON

After hearing that Dr. Thurman had moved into another phase of his existence, I called Dr. Benjamin E. Mays, president emeritus of Morehouse College, who could not be here today because he preached yesterday before the joint session of the South Carolina General Assembly. He could not travel to San Francisco in time. "Dr. Mays," I asked, "what is the point of Howard Thurman?" He said, "Jesse, he generated in the minds of young negroes the idea of freedom. When they saw Howard Thurman, most of them, for the first time, saw a free man. When they heard or read Howard Thurman, for the first time they experienced a free man and this freedom was contagious."

I asked Dr. John Hope Franklin, professor of history at the University of Chicago, "What is the point of this Howard Thurman?" He answered that he gave the philosophical basis, with creative insight, for the self-esteem of the individual, regardless of race, with abiding faith in self and God, and did so with such power that he packed chapels. That was as characteristic of his ministry as long pauses and penetrating stares.

I asked Dr. Mary Frances Barrett, "What of Dr. Thurman?" She said his impact upon students on college campuses was this wise: He went to the heart of things and gave one the feeling and experience of high culture with earthly inspiration. "He was an authentic spirit in the flesh."

As an activist I was attracted to Dr. Thurman, for he always challenged me and mine to move to what he called "the irreducible essence," and I searched for the irreducible essence. It used to embarrass me because I could not give a fast answer to that penetrating challenge. His point was that if you ever developed a cultivated will, with spiritual discipline, the flame of freedom would never perish. The irreducible essence, the cultivated will with spiritual discipline, would never perish.

Dr. Thurman died when he got ready, at his home, with his house in order. It was during Passion Week, on a hill steep like Calvary, without a cross, but with eighty years of black experience—and that is substantially heavy, Dr. Thurman, a freed man who freed other men, one of the tallest trees ever to sprout from the black forest, whose branches hung over the walls and gave shade and protection to the world's lost, whose seed brought forth new trees.

Along with Dr. Mays and Dr. Mordecai Johnson, late president emeritus of Howard University, these three great orators articulated the philosophical bent and scholarship and passion of the black struggle. These men were the barrels of the gun that blew away the philosophical underpinnings of racism and segregation.

Dr. Thurman was a teacher of teachers, a leader of leaders, a preacher of preachers. No small wonder, then, that Martin Luther King Jr., Whitney Young, Samuel Proctor, Vernon E. Jordan, Otis Moss, and those of us who are here today, sat at his feet, for we knew it was a blessing to give this prophet a glass of water or to touch the hem of his garment.

He was black, but he did not wear his blackness as a garment. His ethnicity was self-evident. He did not have to work to be black; he was black without effort; and so he focused beyond ethnicity on that which is ethical, that which is efficient, that which is excellent, that which is essence; for these areas—the ethical, the efficient, the inner essence—required effort.

All of his twenty-one books convinced me that mind can conquer matter, triumph over tragedy, he the eminent theologian, thinker, scholar, dean of Rankin Chapel, dean of March Chapel, this breakthrough at the latter post at Boston University. There was the Jackie Robinson, breaking the sound barrier in the areas of the highest scholarship. Coming from academic discipline with discipline of the spirit, a lasting testimony to the value of black colleges in general and Morehouse in particular. He crowned his alma mater with glory and honor. He sowed the seeds that bred generations of activists who tore down ancient walls of oppression. Howard Thurman was our gallant leader.

He cherished stripping people with penetrating questions: Who are you? And after the five-minute pause, where are you really going, not on the airplane, but where are you going? How are you coming along with that which is irreducible? Dr. Thurman was the "spirit doctor," not with acupuncture that sticks pins into you but with a kind of Thurman-puncture, a kind of spiritual laser beam. Who are you? I know you graduated from a good college. I know you are doing well. I know you have a big church. I see you in the press. I read about you. But, who are you? Without your land, your car, your house, your position, your reputation, your social recognition, all of which is negotiable and transitory. Who are you? What is there about you that remains, that is the irreducible? I am concerned about the integrity and health of your spirit; that must ever remain non-negotiable!

Lastly, who would such a penetrating spirit, scholar, mystic, attract men and women who emerged as political activists, the political leaders of our time? Because, under the black condition you either accommodate or resist; and when you do not have money to resist, or political power, or judicial power, or social respect, you have left only your spirit. And if your spirit is disciplined and determined and your will is cultivated, that is more than enough. He taught that we must let nothing break our spirit. He taught that we cannot determine our oppression, but we can determine our response to it with a disciplined spirit and developed mind. That is the philosophical presupposition of all our civil rights strategies. They may, like Job, take away your things, your family; they may distort, disrupt, bankrupt, discredit. Don't let them have your spirit, which determines your response. They will have their Calvary for you; they cannot determine your response to your Calvary.

The story Dr. Thurman told that impressed me most during my earliest years of friendship with him is one that I used to answer those who have asked, "But what is the connection between this man and this activism, this civil rights, this politics?" He told of walking through the field in Florida with his older sister, who was resisting allowing him to grow up. A snake crawled into the path. She became frightened. He put his bare foot with his full weight on that snake. She became awestruck with his power, accepting of his manhood, but he couldn't stop with that gratification because something more profound had happened. Under all that weight the snake throbbed, and as the snake throbbed the feeling went up his leg. When he flinched and moved his foot only slightly, the snake burst to freedom.

So it is that in spite of all the superiority of the weight on black people, at that moment of our greatest sense of agony, no matter who is in the White House, no matter how far we are from our goal of freedom, if we continue to throb, and to remain sober and sane, and sensitive, and maintain integrity of spirit that is disciplined, then whatever and however the weight adjusts, we will dash to freedom.

The throb of Howard Thurman, his disciplined spirit, his quest for kinship with God, leaves his irreducible essence forever alive. Howard Thurman is experiencing eternal life.

VERNON E. JORDAN, JR.

Ten years ago Howard Thurman gave the eulogy at Whitney Young's funeral. Among his first words were the following: "Whitney Young is dead. This is his fact and our reality." I remember the surge of recognition that ran through the mourners when Howard uttered those words. Few of us had yet come to grips with Whitney's loss, and when Howard in his direct forthright way said the words we all knew were true and yet denied in the deepest recesses of our minds, a wave of relief swept through the church.

The memory is on my mind today along with much else. It reminds me of Howard's ability to blend harsh truth with compassion, reality with faith, and so to transform despair to hope. As we grieve at losing Howard's calm presence and profound wisdom, we glory in the memories he left us, the faith he brought us, and the example of integrity he set for us. I know that Howard's healing gifts helped me overcome my own illness last year. He and I spoke on the telephone every week. I played tapes of his sermons and lectures. I read his inspiring books. Howard helped me overcome. He was my personal pastor, spiritual guide. Howard Thurman was my friend.

So I owe him a debt of gratitude, and so do all people who had the good fortune to know Howard Thurman. To those of us burdened with the troubles of this world, he offered a vision of God's world, a world of peace and faith and hope. Howard Thurman was a great minister, a great preacher. He was also a great poet and writer. He stands with the most profound thinkers and intellectuals of our history. And, at the same time, he stands with the most giving, warm souls of our times. And death shall have no dominion over Howard Thurman and his lasting effect on us, our children, our children's children, on to future generations. We will read his words of wisdom, hear his voice intoning the great truths, and pass his teachings on.

I have been listening to those tapes and reading his words often this past week, and I can but quote again his eulogy for Whitney, so telling and appropriate for Howard himself. Howard said, "The time and the place of a man's life on earth is the time and the place of his body, but the meaning or significance of his life is as far reaching and redemptive as his gifts, his dedication, his response to the demands of his times, the total commitment of his powers can make it."

As so it is of Howard Thurman. The time and the place of his body are ended, but the vast powers he possessed and the commitment and dedication with which he applied them give his life meaning and value far outlasting the transitory moment of his earthly existence.

Howard Thurman will live in our minds and hearts for as long as men treasure truth, justice, compassion, and friendship.

Go Down, Death

JAMES WELDON JOHNSON

James Weldon Johnson was a poet, novelist, journalist, songwriter, attorney, and diplomat. The author of six volumes of poetry, Johnson took as his inspiration the sermons of the black churches for his collection God's Trombones: Seven Negro Sermons in Verse (1927), from which "Go Down Death" is taken. In this poem, the rhythms, fervor, and messages of the old time preacher flow through the lines, creating not only a reminder of the strength inherent in the best sermons, but also providing comfort in the face of the ultimate sorrow, death.

Go Down, Death

Weep not, weep not,
She is not dead;
She's resting in the bosom of Jesus.
Heart-broken husband—weep no more;
Grief-stricken son—weep no more;
Left-lonesome daughter—weep no more;
She only just gone home.

Day before yesterday morning,
God was looking down from his great, high heaven,
Looking down on all his children,
And his eye fell on Sister Caroline,
Tossing on her bed of pain.
And God's big heart was touched with pity,
With the everlasting pity.

And God sat back on his throne,
And he commanded that tall, bright angel standing
    on his right hand:
Call me Death!

And that tall, bright angel cried in a voice
That broke like a clap of thunder:
Call Death!—Call Death!
And the echo sounded down the streets of heaven
Till it reached away back to that shadowy place,
Where Death waits with his pale, white horse.

And Death heard the summons,
And he leaped on his fastest horse,
Pale as a sheet in the moonlight.
Up the golden street Death galloped,
And the hooves of his horses struck fire from the gold,
But they didn't make no sound.
Up Death rode to the Great White Throne,
And waited for God's command.

And God said: Go down, Death, go down,
Go down to Savannah, Georgia,
Down in Yamacraw,
And find Sister Caroline.
She's borne the burden and heat of the day,
She's labored long in my vineyard,
And she's tired—
She's weary—
Go down, Death, and bring her to me.

And Death didn't say a word,
But he loosed the reins on his pale, white horse,
And he clamped the spurs to his bloodless sides,
And out and down he rode,
Through heaven's pearly gates,
Past suns and moons and stars;
on Death rode,

Leaving the lightning's flash behind;
Straight down he came.

Well, we were watching round her bed,
She turned her eyes and looked away,
She saw what we couldn't see;
She saw Old Death. She saw Old Death
Coming like a falling star.
But Death didn't frighten Sister Caroline;
He looked to her like a welcome friend.
And she whispered to us: I'm going home,
And she smiled and closed her eyes.

And Death took her up like a baby,
And she lay in his icy arms,
But she didn't feel no chill.
And Death began to ride again—
Up beyond the evening star,
Into the glittering light of glory,
On to the Great White Throne.
And there he laid Sister Caroline
On the loving breast of Jesus.

And Jesus took his own hand and wiped away her tears,
And he smoothed the furrows from her face,
And the angels sang a little song,
And Jesus rocked her in his arms,
And kept a-saying: Take your rest,
Take your rest.

Weep not—weep not,
She is not dead;
She's resting in the bosom of Jesus.

Transformed Nonconformist

MARTIN LUTHER KING, JR.

Martin Luther King, Jr. is an icon for the struggle for equality in the United State during the twentieth century. Charismatic, intelligent, open, and warm, King moved mountains and audiences with his words. While many only know him from his "I Have A Dream" speech, all of his sermons encapsulate the fervor and caring that characterized his life. In many respects, King combines the best features of the emotive preachers and the learned preachers in his sermons. The result is messages that are timeless, emotional, and powerful; messages that can change the world. As do so many of his sermons, King's "Transformed Nonconformist" criticizes, moves, and guides, seeking to shape and change the lives of those who hear or read it in positive, dynamic ways.

Transformed Nonconformist

B e not conformed to this world: but be ye transformed by the renewing of your mind.

ROMANS 12:2

"DO NOT CONFORM" is difficult advice in a generation when crowd pressures have unconsciously conditioned our minds and feet to move to the rhythmic drumbeat of the status quo. Many voices and forces urge us to choose the path of least resistance, and bid us never to fight for an unpopular cause and never to be found in a pathetic minority of two or three.

Even certain of our intellectual disciplines persuade us of the need to conform. Some philosophical sociologists suggest that morality is merely group consensus and that the folkways are the right ways. Some psychologists say that mental and emotional adjustment is the reward of thinking and acting like other people.

Success, recognition, and conformity are the bywords of the modern world where everyone seems to crave the anesthetizing security of being identified with the majority.

I

In spite of this prevailing tendency to conform, we as Christians have a mandate to be nonconformists. The Apostle Paul, who knew the inner realities of the Christian faith, counseled, "Be not conformed to this world: but be ye transformed by the renewing of your mind." We are called to be people of conviction, not conformity; of moral nobility, not social respectability. We are commanded to live differently and according to a higher loyalty.

Every true Christian is a citizen of two worlds, the world of time and the world of eternity. We are, paradoxically, in the world and yet not of the world. To the Philippian Christians, Paul wrote, "We are a colony of heaven." They, understood what he meant, for their city of Philippi was a Roman colony. When Rome wished to Romanize a province, she established a small colony of people who lived by Roman law and Roman customs and who, though in another country, held fast to their Roman allegiance. This powerful, creative minority spread the gospel of Roman culture. Although the analogy is imperfect-the Roman settlers lived within a framework of injustice and exploitation, that is, colonialism—the Apostle does point to the responsibility of Christians to imbue an unchristian world with the ideals of a higher and more noble order. Living in the colony of time, we arc ultimately responsible to the empire of eternity. As Christians we must never surrender our supreme loyalty to any time-bound custom or earthbound idea, for at the heart of our universe is a higher reality— God and his kingdom of love—to which we must be conformed.

This command not to conform comes, not only from Paul, but also from our Lord and Master, Jesus Christ, the world's most dedicated nonconformist, whose ethical nonconformity still challenges the conscience of mankind.

When an affluent society would coax us to believe that happiness consists in the size of our automobiles, the impressiveness of our houses, and the expansiveness of our clothes, Jesus reminds us, "A man's life consisteth not in the abundance of the things which he possesseth."

When we would yield to the temptation of a world rife with sexual promiscuity and gone wild with a philosophy of self-expression, Jesus tells us that "whosoever looketh on a woman to lust utter her bath committed adultery with her already in his heart."

When we refuse to suffer for righteousness and choose to follow the path of comfort rather than conviction, we hear Jesus say, "Blessed are they which are persecuted for righteousness' sake: for theirs is the kingdom of heaven."

When in our spiritual pride we boast of having reached the peak of moral excellence, Jesus warns, "The publicans and the harlots go into the kingdom of God before you."

When we, through compassionless detachment and arrogant individualism, fail to respond to the needs of the underprivileged, the Master says, "Inasmuch as ye have done it unto one of the least of these my brethren, ye have done it unto file."

When we allow the spark of revenge in our souls to flame up in hate toward our enemies, Jesus teaches, "Love your enemies, bless them that curse you, do good to them that hate you, and pray for them which despitefully use you, and persecute you."

Everywhere and at all times, the love ethic of Jesus is a radiant light revealing the ugliness of our stale conformity.

In spite of this imperative demand to live differently, we have cultivated a mass mind and have moved from the extreme of rugged individualism to the even greater extreme of rugged collectivism. We are not makers of history; we are made by history. Longfellow said, "In this world a man must either be anvil or hammer," meaning that he is either a molder of society or is molded by society. Who doubts that today most men are anvils and are shaped by the patterns of the majority? Or to change the figure, most people, and Christians in particular, are thermometers that record or register the temperature of majority opinion, not thermostats that transform and regulate the temperature of society.

Many people fear nothing more terribly than to take a position which stands out sharply and clearly from the prevailing opinion. The tendency of most is to adopt a view that is so ambiguous that it will include everything and so popular that it will include everybody. Along with this has grown an inordinate worship of bigness. We live in an age of "jumboism" where men find security in that which is large and extensive—big cities, big buildings, big corporations. This worship of size has caused many to tear being identified with a minority idea. Not a few men, who cherish lofty and noble ideals, hide them under a bushel for fear of being called different. Many sincere white people in the South privately oppose segregation and discrimination, but they arc apprehensive lest they be publicly condemned. Millions of citizens arc deeply disturbed that the military-industrial complex too often shapes national policy, but they do not want to be considered unpatriotic. Countless loyal Americans honestly feel that a world body such as the United Nations should include even Red China, but they tear being called Communist sympathizers. A legion of thoughtful persons recognizes that traditional capitalism must continually undergo change if our great national wealth is to be more equitably distributed, but they are afraid their criticisms will make them seem un-American. Numerous decent, wholesome young persons permit themselves to become involved in unwholesome pursuits which they do not personally condone or even enjoy, because they are ashamed to say no when the 'Tang says yes. How fem people have the audacity to express publicly their convictions, and how many have allowed themselves to be "astronomically intimidated!"

Blind conformity makes us so suspicious of an individual who insists on saving what he really believes that we recklessly threaten his civil liberties. If a man, who believes rigorously in peace, is foolish enough to carry a sign in a public demonstration, or it a Southern white person, believing in the American dream of the dignity and worth of human personality, dares to invite a Negro into his home and join with him in his struggle for freedom, he is liable to be summoned before some legislative investigation body. He most certainly is a Communist if he espouses the cause of human brotherhood!

Thomas Jefferson wrote, "I hate sworn upon the altar of God eternal hostility against every form of tyranny over the mind of man." To the conformist and the shapers of the conformist mentality, this must surely sound like a most dangerous and radical doctrine. Have we permitted the lamp of independent thought and individualism to become so dim that were Jefferson to write and live by these words today we would find cause to harass and investigate him? If Americans permit thought-control, business-control, and freedom-control to continue, we shall surely move within the shadows of fascism.

II

Nowhere is the tragic tendency to conform more evident than in the church, an institution which has often served to crystallize, conserve, and even bless the patterns of majority opinion. The erstwhile sanction by the church of slavery, racial segregation, war, and economic exploitation is testimony to the tact that the church has hearkened more to the AUTHORITY of the world than to the authority of God. Called to be the moral guardian of the community' the church at times has preserved that which is immoral and unethical. Called to combat social evils, it has remained silent behind stained-glass windows. Called to lead men on the highway of brotherhood and to summon them to rise above the narrow confines of race and class, it has enunciated and practiced racial exclusiveness.

We preachers have also been tempted by the enticing cult of conformity. Seduced by the success symbols of the world, we have measured our achievements by the size of our parsonage. We have become showmen to please the whims and caprices of the people. We preach comforting sermons and avoid saying anything from our pulpits which might disturb the respectable views of the comfortable members of our congregations. Have we ministers of Jesus Christ sacrificed truth on the altar of self-interest and, like Pilate, yielded our convictions to the demands of the crowd?

We need to recapture the gospel glow of the early Christians, who were nonconformists in the truest sense of the word and refused to shape their witness according to the mundane patterns of the world. Willingly they sacrificed fame, fortune, and life itself in behalf of a cause they knew to be right. Quantitatively small, they were qualitatively giants. Their powerful gospel put an end to such barbaric evils as infanticide and bloody gladiatorial contests. Finally, they captured the Roman Empire for Jesus Christ.

Gradually, however, the church became so entrenched in wealth and prestige that it began to dilute the strong demands of the gospel and to conform to the ways of the world. And ever since the church has been a weak and ineffectual trumpet making uncertain sounds. If the church of Jesus Christ is to regain once more its power, message, and authentic ring, it must conform only to the demands of the gospel.

The hope of a secure and livable world lies with disciplined nonconformists, who are dedicated to justice, peace, and brotherhood. The trailblazers in human, academic, scientific, and religious freedom have always been nonconformists. In any cause that concerns the progress of mankind, put your faith in the nonconformist!

In his essay "Self-Reliance" Emerson wrote, "Whoso would be a man must be a nonconformist." The Apostle Paul reminds us that whoso would be a Christian must also be a nonconformist. Any Christian who blindly accepts the opinions of the majority and in fear and timidity follows a path of expediency and social approval is a mental and spiritual slave. Mark well these words from the pen of James Russell Lowell:

They are slaves who fear to
speak For the fallen and
the weak; They are slaves
who will not choose Hatred,
scoffing, and abuse, Rather
than in silence shrink From
the truth they needs must think;
They are slaves who dare not be
In the right with two or three.

Nonconformity in itself, however, may not necessarily be good and may at times possess neither transforming nor redemptive power. Nonconformity per se contains no saving value, and may represent in some circumstances little more than a form of exhibitionism. Paul in the latter half of the text offers a formula for constructive nonconformity: "Be ye transformed by the renewing of your mind." Nonconformity is creative when it is controlled and directed by a transformed life and is constructive when it embraces a new mental outlook. By opening our lives to God in Christ we become new creatures. This experience, which Jesus spoke of as the new birth, is essential if we are to be transformed nonconformists and treed from the cold hard heartedness and self-righteousness so often characteristic of nonconformity. Someone has said, "I love reforms but I hate reformers." A reformer may be an untransformed nonconformist whose rebellion against the evils of society has left him annoyingly rigid and unreasonably impatient.

Only through an inner spiritual transformation do we gain the strength to fight vigorously the evils of the world in a humble and loving spirit. The transformed nonconformist, moreover, never yields to the passive sort of patience which is an excuse to do nothing. And this very transformation saves him from speaking irresponsible words which estrange without reconciling and from making hasty judgments which are blind to the necessity of social progress. He recognizes that social change will not come overnight, yet he works as though it is an imminent possibility.

This hour in history needs a dedicated circle of transformed non-conformists. Our planet teeters on the brink of atomic annihilation; dangerous passions of pride, hatred, and selfishness are enthroned in our lives; truth lies prostrate on the rugged hills of nameless calvaries; and men do reverence before false gods of nationalism and material-ism. The saving of our world from pending doom will come, not through the complacent adjustment of the conforming majority, but through the creative maladjustment of a nonconforming minority.

Some years ago professor Bixler reminded us of the danger of overstressing the well-adjusted life. Everybody passionately seeks to be well adjusted. We must, of course, be well-adjusted if we are to avoid neurotic and schizophrenic personalities, but there are some things in our world to which men of goodwill must be maladjusted-I confess that I never intend to become adjusted to the evils of seg-regation and flee crippling effects of discrimination, to the moral degeneracy of religious bigotry and the corroding effects of narrow sectarianism, to economic conditions that deprive men of work and food, and to the insanities of militarism and the self-defeating effects of physical violence.

Human salvation lies in the hands of the creatively maladjusted. We need today maladjusted men like Shacirach, Meshlch, and Abednego, who, when ordered by King Nebuchadnezzar to bow before a golden image, said in unequivocal terms, "If it be so, our God whom we serve is able to deliver us . . . . But it not . . . we will not serve thy gods;" like Thomas Jefferson, who in an age adjusted to slavery wrote, "We hold these truths to be self-evident, that all men are created equal, that they are endowed by their Creator with certain unalienable Rights, that among these are life, Liberty and the pursuit of Happiness;" like Abraham Lincoln, who had the wisdom to discern that this nation could not survive halt slave and half free; and supremely like our Lord, who, in the midst of the intricate and fascinating military machinery of the Roman Empire, reminded his disciples that "they that take the sword shall perish with the sword." Through such maladjustment an already decadent generation may be called to those things which make for peace.

Honesty impels me to admit that transformed nonconformity, which is always costly and never altogether comfortable, may mean walking through the valley of the shadow of suffering, losing a job, or having a six-year-old daughter ask, "Daddy, why do you have to go to jail so much?" But we are gravely mistaken to think that Christianity protects us from the pain and agony of mortal existence. Christianity has always insisted that the cross we bear precedes the crown we wear. To be a Christian, one must take up his cross, with all of its difficulties and agonizing and tragedy-packed content, and carry it until that very cross leaves its marks upon us and redeems us to that more excellent way which comes only through suffering.

In these days of worldwide confusion, there is a dire need for men and women who will courageously do battle for truth. We need Christians who will echo the words John Bunyan said to his jailer when, having spent twelve years in jail, he was promised freedom if he would agree to stop preaching:

But if nothing will do, unless I make of my conscience a continual butchery and slaughter-shop, unless, putting out my own eyes, I commit me to the blind to lead me, as I doubt is desired by some, I have determined, the Almighty God being my help and shield, yet to suffer, if frail life might continue so long, even till the moss shall grow on mine eyebrows, rather than thus to violate my faith and principles.

We must make a choice. Will we continue to march to the drumbeat of conformity and respectability, or will we, listening to the beat of a more distant drum, mom to its echoing sounds? Will we march only to the music of time, or will we, risking criticism and abuse, march to the soul-saving music of eternity? Mom than wee before we are today challenged by the words of yesterday, "Be not conformed to this world: but be ye transformed by the renewing of your mind."

A Warrior for Justice:
Eulogy of Adam Clayton Powell, Jr.

SAMUEL DEWITT PROCTOR

Samuel Dewitt Proctor assumed the ministry of the Abyssinian Baptist Church in Harlem, New York, after the resignation and death of its dynamic leader of many years, Adam Clayton Powell, Jr. It was only fitting, therefore, that Proctor deliver a eulogy in Powell's honor. The praise Proctor gives Powell—that "He fought a good fight, he finished his course. He kept the faith"—would apply equally to himself. Until his own death in 1997, Proctor was a tireless fighter for civil rights, and advisor to presidents, and a dedicated teacher and minister. In this eulogy, as he does in many of his sermons, Proctor emphasizes his belief that change is possible if faith is present.

A Warrior for Justice:
Eulogy of Adam Clayton Powell, Jr.

The second Epistle of Timothy is the benedictory of a tired warrior who had come to the end of his days. Paul writes to his young disciple and fellow-laborer, Timothy. Let me paraphrase that Epistle.

He starts by saying, Timothy, I think about you night and day. I remember how you cried when you leaned of my sorrows.

Timothy, I remember the great faith of Lois, your grandmother and of Eunice, your mother. True believers, I remember ordaining you and I hope you will keep your gift alive.

Never be ashamed of being a preacher, Timothy, and don't be ashamed of me because I am in jail for the gospel. Be honored when you can suffer for the gospel.

I do indeed suffer but I am not ashamed: "I know whom I have believed and am persuaded that he is able . . ."

And then, after other admonitions, he said to him, "I am now ready." Ready. "Ready to be offered, and the time of my departure is at hand. I have fought a good fight, I have finished my course, I have kept the faith . . ."

Then he went on and laid his soul bare. He was saying that he didn't mind dying but what he couldn't stand was the loneliness that went before death. He said, Timothy come to see me as soon as you can. Everybody has left me alone. Demas is gone back to Thessalonika, Crescens has gone to Galatia, Titus to Dalmatia. Everybody has left, only Luke has stuck with me. Find John Mark. Bring him with you when you come, and when you come through Troas, pick up a coat and some books I left there at the home of Carpus.

Remember Alexander the coppersmith? He was awfully cruel to me. At my first trial, in fact, no man stood with me. Nobody! But the Lord was by my side and was strengthening me every minute.

Come to see me. Try to get here before winter. But remember . . . I am ready, any time now. "I have fought a good fight. I have finished my course, I have kept the faith."

To the bereaved family, to Skipper, to the officers and members of Abyssinian, to the friends and mourners who have gathered, we are here to bid farewell to another warrior.

I received word shortly after his passing from his devoted friend, Dr. Aaron Wells, and I began immediately to reflect on his enormous contributions.

Later, his trusted associate for many years, Odell Clark, called and as we reviewed some of his victories for the people, hardly have so many people ever owed so much to one man.

Every once in a while history has to clear the way for a giant who is prepared to stride across the stage of time. Once in a generation we can expect a Frederick Douglass, an Adam Powell, or a Martin Luther King Jr., one who is sensitive to injustice, perceptive of institutional evil, and who is prepared to fling himself into confrontation with the forces of oppression.

These men move with selfless abandon because their actions originate with an early response to the call of God. They are propelled by a strange urge from within that is like the feeling that Jeremiah had when he said, "His word was in mine heart as a burning fire shut up in my bones, and I was weary with forbearing and I could not stay."

You see, good religion, like love, is a many splendored thing. It has several manifestations. When the light of God shines in the human soul, it reflects itself prismatically like a diamond with several facets. On one side there is the element of ecstasy, just sheer ecstasy, the feeling of overflowing that makes one cry "Glory!" It made the Psalmist sing, "I will lift up mine eyes unto the hills, whence cometh my help." Overflowing ecstasy.

Ecstasy! It made the prophet Isaiah cry when he had his vision, "Woe is me! For I am undone . . . ." Ecstasy. It made Charles Wesley write, "O, for a thousand tongues to sing, my Great Redeemer's praise!"

Ecstasy. It used to make my grandmother close her eyes and tighten her lips and whisper, "Praise the Lord!" That is one side of religion.

On another side we find simplicity, getting life uncluttered, withdrawal from the world, asceticism, contemplation, and serenity. This is what religion means to some. The simple, quiet life.

Saint Francis, for example, was born the son of a cloth merchant and became an ascetic. He was of noble lineage. As a young soldier-adventurer he joined one crusade after another until a vision obsessed him. He gave himself to solitude and prayer. He renounced his wealth and went in rags, mingling with the beggars and asking alms. When he tried to seize his father's wealth and give it away, he was arrested.

Having adopted a life of poverty and simplicity, he organized a new order, the Franciscans, with 12 disciples and won the approval of Pope Innocent III.

Now, let's face it, the simple life of poverty and withdrawal does have its rewards. From such living, enormous spiritual wealth can accrue. Listen to the prayer of Saint Francis, for example:

> "O Lord
> Make me an instrument of thy peace,

Where there is Hatred let me sow love,
Where there is injury, pardon,
Where there is darkness, light,
Where there is sadness, joy,
Where there is doubt, faith,
And where there is despair, hope.

O Divine Master,
Grant that I may not so much seek
To be consoled as to console,
To be understood as to understand,
To be loved as to love.

For
It is in giving that we receive,
It is in forgiving that we are pardoned,
And it is in dying that we are born to eternal life."

On another side we find charity, pure altruism, self-giving. This has always been an important criterion of good religion.

When John the Baptist sent his followers to ask Jesus for his credentials, Jesus sent word back to John: charity! Meeting human needs!

The blind see,
The lame walk,
The lepers are cleansed,
The deaf hear.

It doesn't make any difference if you can move a mountain, feed the poor . . . nothing. You need real charity! He said that the things that will last the longest are faith, hope, and charity, but the greatest is charity.

The list could be longer, but the only other side of good religion that calls for attention today is justice. In the earliest documents of the Old Testament, we find a craving for justice.

When Nathan the prophet found David the king wrong, in the name of justice, he told him, "Thou art the man."

Justice is that human virtue that does not wait for volitional, spontaneous, unscheduled charity, Justice says that a certain kind of fair play should be counted on, expected, scheduled and without which some penalty is sure to follow.

Justice says that if you plan to do right, write it down, tell everybody, make it known, commit yourself, let us all be in on it together. Justice is blind, impartial, persistent, evenhanded, plays no favorites.

The prophet Micah said that this was among the highest priorities of religion. He said, "What doth the Lord require of thee, but to do justly, to love mercy and to walk humbly with God."

The prophet Amos gave it an even higher priority. He said that God would not listen to their violin music or be deceived by the sweet fragrance of their incense. He said, "Let justice roll down as waters, and righteousness as a mighty stream."

Jesus applied the principles of justice when he found people eager to judge the lives of others. He said you can't see a mote in your brother's eye if you have a big splinter in your own. When they wanted to stone a woman to death who was alleged to be unfaithful, he asked the one who had no sin at all to cast the first stone.

Justice. It is an ancient concept found in the Code of Hammurabi 2,000 years before Christ, but a very simple one. It says don't ask a privilege for yourself that you would not grant to everyone similarly situated. On the other hand, it says don't do to another person what you would not want done to you. It is even-handedness.

But my friends, lying behind the notion of justice is the assumption that someone will be around to see that it is done, to supervise it, to monitor it, to guarantee it, to give it force. There just has to be someone who has the fine tuning, the understanding to know when a situation is out of balance, and that somebody must have the courage, the brains, the audaciousness, the cool bravery, and the passionate zeal, the size, the voice, the looks, the energy, the following to force an issue in the name of justice.

This is where the work and the ministry of Adam Clayton Powell, Jr. comes to the fore. If Charles Wesley was a man of ecstasy, if St. Francis was a man of simplicity; if St. Paul was a man of charity; then Adam Powell stands in the train of Amos and Micah who were men of justice.

In 1941, when Adam Clayton Powell, Jr. was elected to the City Council of New York City, I was a college senior in Virginia. I was proud of my progress and I was burdened with ambition. The campus of Virginia Union University, where his father received his education, was located on a hill on the edge of the north end of Richmond. We reveled in our youthful exuberance in that Confederate citadel, and we were inspired by our Black heroes. Adam Powell, Jr. was our new hero. He had defied the power structure, had created a black political base, and had given us our first evidence that American institutions were capable of any change at all.

This new fact that he flashed before us burned itself into the consciousness of a young college boy. I had no assurance at all that my degree, my sacrifices, my new learning would be an avenue to success or to freedom. We lived behind a thick wall of segregation. There was no hint of change in 1941. The churches were segregated, the unions were segregated, the colleges and universities were segregated, the hospitals and cemeteries, restaurants and hotels, buses and trains—in every way possible my country screamed at me making me think I was nobody, in 1941. But Adam Clayton Powell, Jr. was marching up and down Seventh Avenue telling us we were somebody.

That was the beginning of one of the most colorful and significant careers that any man has had in the twentieth century. We pause today to bid him farewell as the dream closes, the curtain falls, the lights grown dim, and the script is finished.

Come now and see that as a prophet of social justice he put the plight of the urban black and poor on the nation's agenda as no one had done before.

Our problems remain so largely unsolved. But no one can deny that the plight of the urban poor—the black poor—is before the attention of America. And those who know the history will remember that it was Adam Powell who brought the issue out in the open, carried it to City Hall and then on to Washington.

President Johnson and President Kennedy wrote him letters and thanked him for handling the work of the House Committee on Education and Labor more productively than any other chairman had ever done. The major social legislation of both Kennedy and Johnson had to go through that committee and there had not been any social legislation at all in the hundred years before.

What do we owe to Adam? Federal man-power training, Head Start, Job Corps, higher minimum wage, federal aid to education, loans for college students and federal dollars for school equipment, new training for Indians, new help for migrant laborers, new opportunities for the handicapped, the deaf, the blind, the aged and the mentally retarded.

In other words, that entire procession of persons whom Jesus met on the hills of Judea and on the road through Samaria and around the Sea of Galilee, all of those who had been beaten and broken by poverty and disease, whose lives were being snuffed out slowly by steady oppression—that's the crowd of persons in modern terms who were on Adam's mind. He roared like a lion and snapped like a cobra in their defense.

Come further and see that as a prophet of social justice he awakened with a one-sided version of Christianity. We paid a lot of attention to the minutia of religion. Who would be baptized, who could take communion, how to debate on the Bible, who could be saved, etc. We were reared around Southern Methodists, Episcopalians, and Baptists. They kept us singing about heaven with our condition on earth unchanged. They had rigid teachings about Christ but they forgot the teachings of Christ. It all had to do with his birth and death, but they forgot entirely about his life.

Nevertheless, the black churches played an indispensable role. Men like Adam Powell, Jr. had the ability to bring people together, to inspire them to improve their lot and to protect their gains. Dr. Powell, Jr. was one of the real champions of the people in New Haven and in New York. His fiery preaching caused the hearts of men to be strangely warmed and after the respite of the Sabbath they could return to face a week of hard work.

They were also educated in civic and political affairs by the pastors. An organized social action, coming out of the sanctuary to face the enemy of righteousness—that was something new. And it made all the difference. His work helped to insure that it would be acknowledged that social justice was nothing more than the gospel applied to modern life. He began a tradition that later spawned Leon Sullivan, Channing Phillips, Walter Fauntroy, Wyatt Tee Walker, Andrew Young, Ralph Abernathy, Jesse L. Jackson, and many others. Of course, Martin Luther King, Jr. was his prized progeny. This church, Abyssinian, and her officers and members, deserve the highest praise for standing by him with unfailing loyalty.

Finally, as a prophet of social justice he followed a long and lonely path. When a man is burdened with a passion to ameliorate social conditions, he steps on a lot of tender feelings, like romping through a bed or roses. The petals fall on all sides.

Every time he made a move he scared away another group of friends. Every time he lifted his voice in defense of one group, it was an offense to another. Follow that program for 35 years and see what it gets you—loneliness, enemies, detractors, and false friends. So many people are beholden to the power structure that when you make relentless assaults upon it you shake a lot of friends loose. Your cause becomes too risky. Jesus lost his family, his followers, and finally his closest colleague, Simon Peter.

Adam Powell, Jr. was the first black leader in America whose financial support came from the people he served. His money was indigenous. Homegrown. Right here. And he was therefore free to speak his mind, and this did not make him friends among those in power.

He took out after the dime stores, the hospitals, the department store, the telephone company, the City of New York, the State of New York, the labor unions, the construction industry, the colleges and universities, and the United States Marine Corps. He was unafraid. The chemistry of defiance was in his blood and he responded to it until he was weakened by illness.

But each of these battles caused his enemies to vow that at the right time they would make their assault.

When he was denied a chance to take his congressional seat, it was one of the most blatant examples of a double standard and of the height of contempt for bold black men that the nation has seen. The men who excluded him had sat in the House for years allowing racism to run rampant, subsidizing their favorite industries at the expense of the poor, denying Constitutional rights to black people, maintaining segregation in Washington, D.C., allowing the states to go to any lengths to deny black people rights, giving grants to contractors who discriminated against black folks, giving money to hospitals who didn't allow black doctors to practice, and giving money to universities that didn't allow black folks to study. They supported a segregated Army, Navy, Air Force, National Guard, FBI, and State Police.

Adam took out after the whole crowd. He threw down the foul flag every time he saw one. They couldn't stand him so they tightened the noose, and when they thought they had him, they sprang the trap.

All this he did, remember now, for a people who had been in the country for 350 years and who were only half free. It was our cause that he gave himself to serve. Life is vastly different today because of his valiant fight on our behalf.

Like St. Paul, facing his end, he came down to the shore of time a lonesome man.

But as St. Paul said to Timothy, I can hear Adam answering the moment. "I am not ashamed. I know whom I have believed, and he is able . . ."

"The time of my departure is at hand. I have fought a good fight, I have finished my course, I have kept the faith."

Farewell, Adam. We'll never forget you. You made a big difference among us. God speed you on your journey. You don't want us to weep, but parting is such sweet sorrow.

But Adam, our sorrow is assuaged by one strong truth that won't let us go. Although you depart from us alone and leave for the other shore, lost from sight in the dim horizon, somehow we can't help but believe that Jesus was right when he said that in our Father's house there were many mansions. You won't be alone, Adam.

In that land of sweet forever, where the wicked cease from troubling and the weary are at rest, you will find other arrivals who have left just a little while ago. There is a great company whom we have bidden farewell, who wait for you on the other side! Medgar Evers from Jackson is there; Whitney Young just left; young Mike King is there; Ralph Bunche hasn't been long gone. You'll find others there, Adam. Malcolm has made the journey. There are more.

John said he saw a hundred and forty-four thousand who sang a new song. No One could sing the song but the hundred and forty-four thousand whom God had redeemed from the earth.

He fought a good fight, he finished his course. He kept the faith.

Keep the Faith, Baby!

ADAM CLAYTON POWELL, JR.

Adam Clayton Powell, Jr. was perhaps one of the most contro-
versial religious leaders of modern times. A minister of the
prestigious Abyssinian Baptist Church in New York City, as his father
was before him, Powell was also elected to congress in 1944, where
he served amidst controversy until 1968. It is easy to understand who
voters kept reelecting Powell and his parishioners steadfastly defended
him despite the scandals that seemed to plague him when one reads
his sermons, for Powell was a charismatic leader and speaker. This is
clearly seen in this sermon. Like the rousing, old-time "exhorters,"
the slave preachers of long ago, Powell emotionally urges his listeners
to "Keep the faith," despite the inequities the see about them, and he
calls upon them to ever seek the truth.

Keep the Faith, Baby!

Keep the faith, baby!

As I walk the streets of the Harlems of the world, the black Harlems and the white Harlems, people are depressed. They are frustrated, they are downtrodden. They see no hope, they see no tomorrows. And I say to them always, Keep the faith, baby!

I say this because all over the world people are not receiving God. They're not getting the assurances that once were given. Promises have been broken, and their dawn refuses to rise. They're walking in the midnights of sorrow, in the midnight of frustration, in the midnight of despair. Too long have they been promised the good life by the great white fathers. Too long have they waited in vain, black and white, poor and illiterate, for the better jobs, better housing, better education, better hospitals. Yet the conditions have not changed, except for those who have always lived in the penthouses. For the people who live in the basements and the cellar, their lives are still drab, ugly. They have no hope, and I say to them, Keep the faith, baby!

Keep the faith! Because God's realities always exceed man's fondest dreams. Keep faith in God, whoever your God is! Keep the faith in whatever God you believe in, keep the faith. He'll take care of things, He'll make a way out of no way, He'll open doors that no one can open and shut doors that no one can shut. And it won't be long before He proves it, too. Keep the faith in yourself! You may be small to your oppressors, but you're bigger in your self-respect as a human being because as a human being nobody is better than you are.

All human beings, black and white, rich and poor, are equal in the sight of God. Keep your faith in the life of your fellow man even though he abuses you. When he abuses you, he makes himself a lesser man. A great man once said, "Love your enemies, bless them that curse you, do good to them that hate you, and pray, pray, pray, pray, pray for them which will use you and persecute you." Keep your faith! Keep your faith because once day, black and white, Jew and gentile, Protestant and Catholic, rich and poor, are going to walk the face of this earth with joyful hearts, happy in the togetherness of brotherhood. And the masses are going to run this world. The big man's day is gone, not only because it is any man's world, but it's also and always has been and always will be God's world.

Keep the faith, keep the faith, baby, oh, for a fate that will not shrink, oppressed by any foe, that will not tremble upon the brink of any earthly woe. Keep your faith, baby! Walk together, talk together, love together, worship together, live together, and we'll win tomorrow! Because God has no other hands, than our hands, he has no other feet than our feet, and he has no other tongue than our tongue.

Keep the faith, keep the faith, baby!

About the Contributors

MAYA ANGELOU

A poet, educator, historian, bestselling author, actress, playwright, civil-rights activist, producer, and director, Dr. Maya Angelou is one of the great voices of contemporary literature. Among her 11 bestselling books are I Know Why the Caged Bird Sings and Even The Stars Look Lonesome.

LERONE BENNETT, JR.

Journalist, historian, and writer Lerone Bennett, Jr. is executive editor of Ebony magazine. He is the author of Before the Mayflower: a History of Black America and seven other books. He lives in Chicago, Illinois.

KATIE G. CANNON

Katie Geneva Cannon is the first African-American woman to be ordained to the ministry in the United Presbyterian Church in the United States and the first African-American woman to earn the Doctor of Philosophy degree from Union Theological Seminary in New York. She is Associate Professor of Religion at Temple University in Philadelphia and previously taught at Episcopal Divinity School in Cambridge, Massachusetts. Dr. Cannon is the author of Black Womanist Ethics and Katie's Canon: Womanism and the Soul of the Black Community.

REV. SHARONE DAVIS-SMITH

Sharone Davis-Smith was born in Jersey City, New Jersey. She entered into the ministry at the age of sixteen and was educated at Kean University and Virginia Union University's School of Theology. She is currently the youth pastor at Bible-Based Fellowship Church of Temple Terrace in Tampa, Florida. She and her husband, Arthur W. Smith, Jr., have a three-year-old daughter, Heaven.

C.L. FRANKLIN

Clarence LaVaughn (C.L.) Franklin was born in 1915 in rural Mississippi and attended Lemoyne College in Memphis, Tennessee. Known by many as the father of Aretha Franklin, he became pastor of the New Bethel Church in Detroit in 1946 and quickly became one of the greatest soul preachers in history. He toured and recorded extensively, releasing dozens of albums of sermons and gospel songs. His influence is still felt today in the modern-day evangelists and revivalists like Jasper Williams, Jr. and C.L. Moore. He was shot during an attempted burglary in 1979 and remained in a light coma for five years until his death in 1984.

JAMES HASKINS

Dr. James Haskins is one of the world's foremost experts on African-American cultural history. A professor of English at the University of Florida, he lives in Gainesville and New York City. He is the author notably of Bricktop, Mr. Bojangles: The Biography of Bill Robinson, The Cotton Club, Mabel Mercer: A Life, and Black Music in America.

JESSE L. JACKSON

The Reverend Jesse L. Jackson, Sr. is president of the Rainbow Coalition and has served as president of Operation PUSHand director of SCLC Operation Bread Basket. One of the leading this country's leading African-American political, religious, and social leaders, he was a candidate for the office of President of the United States in 1984.

JAMES WELDON JOHNSON

James Weldon Johnson was born in 1871 in Jacksonville, Florida. He attended Atlanta University with the intention that the education he received there would be used to further the interests of the black people. In 1900, he wrote the song "Lift Ev'ry Voice and Sing" which became known as the "Negro National Anthem." In 1912, Johnson published The Autobiography of an Ex-Colored Man.

ABSALOM JONES

Absalom Jones (1746-1818) was born a house slave in Delaware. He taught himself to read out of the New Testament and other books. At twenty, he married another slave, purchased her freedom with his earnings, and bought his own freedom in 1784. At St. George's Methodist Episcopal Church, he served as lay minister for its black membership and helped organize the Free African Society, the first organized African-American society in America. In 1792, Jones was ordained as the first African-American deacon of the Episcopal Church.

ANNE DEVEREAUX JORDAN

Anne Devereaux Jordan earned B.A. and M.A. degrees at the University of Michigan. The author of nine books, she founded the Children's Literature Association in 1972 and is a professor of children's literature at Eastern Connecticut State University.

VERNON E. JORDAN, JR.

Vernon E. Jordan, Jr. attended segregated Atlanta schools in the 1940s and early 1950s, then graduated from DePauw University and earned his J.D. at Howard University. He has served as field director of the NAACP, executive director of the National Urban League, and director of the United Negro College Fund, and was a special advisor to President Bill Clinton. His memoirs, Vernon Can Read!, was published to great acclaim in 2001.

MARTIN LUTHER KING, JR.

Martin Luther King, Jr. was born in Atlanta, Georgia, in 1929 and was educated at Morehouse College, Crozer Theological Seminary, and Boston University. While in Montgomery, Alabama, in 1955, Dr. King led a bus boycott to protest the arrest of Rosa Parks, a black woman who would not give up her seat to a white person. Though he was arrested, jailed, and threatened, and his home was bombed, he persevered; in 1956, the Supreme Court ordered the de-segregation of all public transportation. Dr King went on to head the historic Million-Man March in Washington, D.C., on August 28, 1963, where he delivered his extraordinary "I Have a Dream" speech. He was awarded the Nobel Peace Prize the next year. On April 4, 1968, he was assassinated in Memphis, Tennessee. The third Monday in January is now a national holiday in his memory.

C.C. LOVELACE

Very little, if anything, is known about Reverend C. C. Lovelace. His influence endures thanks to Zora Neale Hurston, one of this century's major American writers, who transcribed a sermon he delivered in Eau Gallie, Florida, in 1929.

CAROL ANN NORTH

Carol Ann North is a native of San Antonio, TX. She earned her M.D. at Princeton Theological Seminary. She currently serves as a minister at Third Street Church of God and teaches English and language arts at Benjamin Tasker Middle School in Washington, DC. An accomplished singer, she combines her skills in singing, theater arts, teaching, and preaching to inspire academic and personal excellence in the lives of young people.

ADAM CLAYTON POWELL, JR. (1908-1972)

Adam Clayton Powell, Jr. was born in New Haven, Connecticut, in 1908. He graduated from Colgate University, Columbia University, and the theological department of Shaw University, Raleigh, N.C. A famed teacher, minister, and administrator, he was cofounder of the National Negro Congress and served in Congress from 1945 to 1967 and 1969 to 1971.

SAMUEL DEWITT PROCTOR

Samuel DeWitt Proctor was the grandson of slaves. A renowned theologian, educator at Rutgers, Vanderbilt, Duke, and Yale, and former associate director of the Peace Corps, he succeeded Adam Clayton Powell, Jr. as pastor of Harlem's Abyssinian Baptist Church in 1972 and served until his retirement from the pastorate in 1989. He is the author of numerous books, including The Young Negro in America, My Moral Odyssey, How Shall They Hear?, and The Substance of Things. He died on May 29, 1997.

W. FRANKLYN RICHARDSON II

W. Franklyn Richardson II is Senior Pastor of the 4,000-member Grace Baptist Church in Mt. Vernon, New York, He is a graduate of Virginia Union University, Yale Divinity School and holds a doctorate from United Theological Seminary in Dayton, Ohio. Dr. Richardson is married to the former Inez Nunnally, and they are the parents of two children, Orchid Richardson-Burnside and W. Franklyn Richardson, III.

GARDNER C. TAYLOR

Gardner C. Taylor was born in Louisiana in 1918. He was educated at Leland College and the Oberlin Graduate School of Theology. He is pastor emeritus of the Concord Baptist Church of Christ, Brooklyn New York (1948-1990). The author of four books and numerous articles, he has received many honors, including the Presidential Medal of Freedom, the nation's highest civilian honor, awarded by former President Bill Clinton.

REV. WYATT TEE WALKER

Wyatt Tee Walker holds an earned doctorate from Colgate Rochester Divinity School in African-American studies with a specialization in music. He is the author of twenty-one books, including Common Thieves and The Millennium End Papers. Dr. Walker is a former chief of staff to Dr. Martin Luther King, pulpit minister of the Abyssinian Baptist

Church and special assistant to Governor Nelson Rockefeller. He has been the senior pastor and CEO of the Canaan Baptist Church of Christ since September 1967. Walker is married to the former Theresa Ann Edwards of Washington D.C. They are parents of four adult children and grandparents of two girls.

FREDERICK BOYD WILLIAMS

Frederick Boyd Williams received his B.A. at Morehouse College and a doctorate at Colgate-Rochester Divinity School; D.C.L. He has been the rector of the Episcopal Church of the Intercession in Harlem since 1972. He serves as chairman of the board of Harlem Congregations for Community Improvement and as chairman or trustee of almost every major African-American performing arts group in New York City. He is also an advisor to Archbishop Desmond Tutu and is greatly involved in the AIDS cause in America, Africa and Cuba.

JASPER WILLIAMS, JR.

Jasper Williams, Jr. was born in Memphis, Tennessee, in 1943. The recipient of many awards and honors, including the Rev. C.L. Franklin Masters Award and the NAACP Award, Pastor Williams has served on the Board of numerous service organizations and chaired the Evangelistic Committee's "Late Night Services" under the auspices of the National Baptist Convention USA. Inc. He is pastor of Salem Baptist Church East and West in Atlanta, Georgia.

JEREMIAH A. WRIGHT, JR.

Dr. Jeremiah A. Wright, Jr. was born in Philadelphia, Pennsylvania. He earned a doctorate of ministry from United Theology Seminary and M.A. degrees from Howard University and the University of Chicago. Author, musician, lecturer, and community leader, Dr. Wright is the recipient of three U.S. Presidential Commendations and numerous other awards, including the Proctor Fellow Award and the Rockefeller Fellowship. He is married to the Reverend Ramah Wright, and they have five children and three grandchildren.

CREDITS

All efforts have been made to correctly attribute and contact the copyright holders for the material used in this book. Welcome Rain regrets if any omissions have occurred and will correct any such errors in future editions of this book.

Jasper Williams, Jr., "A Good Soldier: A Eulogy of Clarence LaVaughn (C.L.) Franklin": Used with permission of the author.

AUDIO CREDITS

James Weldon Johnson, "Go Down Death": Read by James Earl Jones, is taken from the International Poetry Forum radio series, produced by WDUQ-FM, Pittsburgh, PA. This nationally distributed public radio series was supported by the Pennsylvania Humanities Council—the Federal-State Partner of the National Endowment for the Humanities; TRACO—The Windows and Doors that Greet the World; and the Buhl Foundation. Special thanks to Mr. Jones for his permission to reproduce his glorious reading.

Jeremiah A. Wright, Jr., "A Broken Life": Courtesy of Jeremiah A. Wright, Jr.

C.L. Franklin, "The Eagle Stirreth Her Nest": From The Eagle Stirreth Her Nest by C.L. Franklin. Copyright © 1984 by MCA Records and Universal Music enterprises.

Gardner C. Taylor, "Jesus Is the Centerpiece of Our Faith": Courtesy of Gardner C. Taylor.

Wyatt Tee Walker, "Choose Ye This Day": Courtesy of Wyatt Tee Walker.

W. Franklyn Richardson II, "What Do the Ashes Say?": Courtesy of W. Franklyn Richardson II.

Adam Clayton Powell, Jr., "Keep the Faith, Baby!" Copyright © 1967 by Adam Clayton Powell, Jr. Courtesy of Adam Clayton Powell IV.

Katie G. Cannon, "Living the Life of Jubilee": Courtesy of Katie G. Cannon.

Jasper Williams, Jr., "A Good Soldier: Eulogy of C.L. Franklin": Courtesy of Jasper Williams, Jr.

The introductions to the sermons are read by the Reverend Sharone Davis-Smith.

PHOTO CREDITS

All contributor photos in the book appear courtesy of the respective contributors, except for C.L. Franklin, which appears courtesy of Jasper Williams, Jr.